Hinduism

The Basics: 4

Hinduism

Herbert Ellinger

SCM PRESS LTD
Trinity Press International

Translated by John Bowden from the German *Hinduismus,*
published 1989 in the *kurz und bündig* series by
hpt-Verlagsgesellschaft m.b.H & Co KG, Vienna.

© hpt-Verlagsgesellschaft m.b.H & Co KG, Vienna 1989

Translation © John Bowden 1995

First U.S. edition published 1996
by Trinity Press International, P.O. Box 851, Valley Forge, PA 19482-0851.

Library of Congress Cataloging-in-Publication Data Available.

ISBN 1-56338-161-3 (Trinity Press)

First British edition published 1995 by SCM Press Ltd, 9-17 St. Albans Place,
London N1 0NX

Typeset at The Spartan Press Ltd, Lymington, Hants

96 97 98 99 00 01 02   8 7 6 5 4 3 2 1

Contents

The World of the Sanatana Dharma

Quite apart from the many millions of people outside the Indian sub-continent who direct their lives in accordance with the principles of the world of Hindu thought, around 550 million Hindus live within the frontiers of the present Republic of India alone. If we assume that no really effective system of birth control can be achieved in the immediate future, the number of people who direct their lives by the sanatana dharma, the 'eternal law', as the Indians call their religion, will increase very rapidly. The same holds for other countries, like Nepal, Bangladesh and Indonesia. So we can assume that by the middle of the first century of the third millennium approximately one billion people will be Hindus.

Today, India itself stands between two conflicting worlds. On the one hand the Hindus are rooted in an age-old tradition and culture which goes back more or less uninterruptedly for 3,500 years, and on the other hand they are on the threshold of what we call the technological age. The Indians have set up industrial centres, they make use of nuclear energy, and in all probability they already possess nuclear weapons. But eighty per cent of people live 'on the land', without machines, without telephones, virtually without any modern technology or comforts in the Western sense. These many small villages are self-contained worlds with age-old rules and laws of life which are strictly laid down in the sanatana dharma ('the eternal law'). So their world-view, which seems diametrically opposed to ours at many points, is called the 'eternal law'. Modern Indians may regard the many centuries of the old caste system as a thing of the past, but out there in the countless villages and small market towns of this gigantic sub-continent it governs life as it always has done. There – though only in isolated instances – suttee, the burning of widows, is still practised. It is not all that long since a report circulated which was difficult to understand, indeed incredible: widows were protesting loudly against the fact that the Indian authorities were imposing severe punishments on cases of suttee.

By far the majority of Indians live under the conditions of village life, which is closely bound to the Hindu tradition. By contrast, the structure of life in the monstrous Indian cities is quite different in many respects. Bombay and Calcutta are gigantic conglomerations. Reports about the size of the population of these cities can only be vague estimates; exact information is probably impossible.

If the sheer amount of distress and what by our standards is the catastrophically low standard of living of most people in country areas already makes an impact on us Westerners, the cruel plight of those living in the urban slums is even more shattering. And the submission, the humility, with which Indians almost always accept their fate is almost incomprehensible to us. As we shall see, this has absolutely nothing to do with the Islamic concept of kismet. Quite different categories of thought allow these people to bear their lot without arguing against it.

Of course we also see well-dressed people, often in European clothing, on the streets of many cities. We will often note that they speak fluent English and have had a completely 'Western education'. But that does not rule out the possibility that someone with a college education will be wearing under his shirt with its European cut the Brahman thread which indicates that he is a member of the highest caste. It is simply that a tradition which came into being many centuries ago, even among enlightened and educated people, is still powerfully alive, but often in a different form.

This sub-continent with its masses of people – which are growing so massively – must find a viable way out of the dilemma sketched out here between age-old traditions and the life-style of the modern industrial age. However, this will be far from easy, and a vast amount in 'tuition fees' will have to be paid.

How do these people – above all those living in country areas – think and feel? How do they regard themselves? How do they see the world into which they have been born? If we assume that in India alone at least 550 million people are living, in the space age, according to the rules of the 'eternal law', the santana dharma, then this cannot be a matter of indifference to us Westerners. The times have changed fundamentally. Whereas only a few decades ago interest in a 'distant land' was motivated essentially by the possibilities of exploiting it, today we have to learn to understand other ways of thinking and other attitudes. People today are no longer objects of exploitation; they can and should be our partners in the family of peoples of our planet.

How around 700 million people understand themselves and the world cannot be a matter of indifference to us Westerners. Today Hinduism stands between age-old traditions which govern human life and the demands of a society which must be part of the modern technological age.

2

The 'Wheel of Rebirth' – The Basis of Hindu Self-Understanding

We shall only be able to understand the Indian attitude to life if we accept that Hindus necessarily find the view that we are given only one life incomprehensible – indeed illogical and paradoxical. Hindus see all the processes of the world we can know – including their lives – as cycles and never as straight lines. Lives do not end, but keep recurring in accordance with clear laws. Hindus see themselves embedded in this cyclical system of the cosmos, the universe.

If we take a brief look at the thousands of years of Hindu history, we shall be struck by the fact that this strong 'trunk' has constantly produced more or less strong 'branches' – Buddhism, Jainism and the Sikhs, to mention only a few. One thing is common to all of these: they have taken over and developed the fundamental idea of the wheel of rebirth. (At this point it should be mentioned that these 'branches' of Hinduism have developed essentially for social and political reasons. We shall go into this when discussing the caste system.)

In order to have some idea of the thought underlying the bhava chakra – the 'wheel of rebirth' – we must familiarize ourselves with some terms from Hindu doctrine, without which we shall not be able to understand it.

Dharma

The Hindu sees dharma as an absolute, cosmic law which governs all processes in the universe – including the life of the individual. So dharma is a very complex term which stands for 'everything that makes up true being'. Thus dharma is also the basis of any human morality and ethics; it is the regularity of all processes in nature and ultimately of the whole cosmos. Dharma is a more or less abstract term which is not directly personified either: dharma is not a god.

We shall be discussing in a later chapter the world of the Hindu gods, which seems so complicated to us.

In attempting to define dharma I have quite deliberately avoided the term 'divine law', which is often used. It seems to carry with it the danger of misunderstanding, since – as we shall discover – the Hindu definition of God is essentially different from ours.

Dharma also stands for the concept of absoluteness postulated in Hinduism, that sphere which is a worthwhile goal for human beings, who belong to the sphere of relativity, but which is ultimately closed to them.

Karma

This key term of Hindu thought can best be understood as an inexorable law of causality: any action, any deed, any activity inevitably results in further actions, further deeds and further activities. This principle of causality also has a negative aspect: any omission to act and so on is necessarily also woven into the network of cause and effect, and this also applies to thoughts – and lack of thought.

It should be quite firmly emphasized here that karma has nothing in common with the Islamic concept of kismet, since karma can be shaped by any individual. It is also striking that grace as defined in Christianity has no place in the Hindu notion of karma. Karma can be shaped by any individual, but it cannot be changed from 'outside'.

The web of karma – the interplay of cause and effect – is the field of tension against which lives are played out. This web is the cause – as it were the potential energy – of samsara, the cycle of birth, life, death and rebirth. So the Hindu inevitably finds a single life as in our Western conception both illogical and impossible. Our idea, which is rooted in the Hebrew Bible, the Christian Old Testament, sees the individual human life as a straight line to God. The Hindu understands things quite differently. Lives form a cycle, and the field of tension between cause and effect is incarnated time and again; it is reborn within the 'wheel of life' until the potential energy of the web of karma is dissipated. This statement also already describes the fundamental aim of human beings from a Hindu perspective: their task is to 'improve' – or better dissolve – their karma until in the end after many lives the goal has been reached: the identity of karma with the absolute law of dharma. In the sphere of the Absolute, rebirths are superfluous.

Moksha and nirvana

The Hindu view of the purpose of human life sketched out above brings us to a thought-world which is particularly difficult for us Westerners to get into. Two abstractions need to be explained, moksha and nirvana.

By moksha the Hindu understands the final liberation and redemption from all worldly ties, from karma and the cycle of birth and death: union with the ultimate reality. Thus the attainment of moksha is the sole purpose of the spiritual quest.

Now to the term nirvana, which is more common in the West. The Sanskrit word nirvana means 'extinguish', and so

Hinduism is constantly termed a 'religion of extinction'. However, this is open to a considerable amount of mis-understanding, since it implies that what is aimed at is 'non-being'. In order to understand the conceptual content of nirvana somewhat better, we must look much more closely at absoluteness and relativity in Hindu thought; here we must be aware that we are using not only our own language but also our own categories of thought. So we shall only achieve very approximate definitions of concepts.

In the Hindu view, all manifestations within the universe which are accessible to our senses – including our capacity to think – are relative; in other words, in absolute terms they are 'untrue'. So Indians call them maya, which could be translated 'deception', illusion. All phenomena in this sphere are subject to polarity, duality, opposition. Life and death are opposites only in the relative sphere, as are light and darkness, good and evil, male and female and so on. So duality is necessarily a characteristic of the sphere of the relative, which is accessible to our senses. Now the Absolute no longer knows any polarity, which is therefore of no relevance. And in Hindu thinking nirvana is connected with the Absolute. Consequently the question of being or non-being can no longer be put, but has become meaningless.

Thus nirvana is not a 'place' nor a 'heaven'. It is thought of as a condition in the sphere of the Absolute without polarities, and therefore the question of being and non-being is without significance.

The term nirvana, which in the Bhagavad Gita is called Brahman-nirvana, can also be found in Buddhism. The differences between the two terms lie in the philosophical sphere and are not important for us here.

At this point I should also point out that there are differences between the thought categories of the spiritual elites and those of ordinary people from lower castes. But this basic framework of thought is common to all Hindus.

The life of the Hindu is governed by ideas of dharma, the absolute law; karma, the causal chain; and the illusory nature of the phenomena accessible to the senses: rebirth through the web of causality and final dissolution in nirvana.

3

The World of the Hindu Gods

Someone once set out to count the Hindu gods. He arrived at 3.3 million. How this man counted the gods and how he arrived at this number he has not told us. I do not want to attempt such a count, nor could I make one. My purpose is to mention the most important and to make an attempt to understand at least the basic features of this pantheon and so enter more deeply into the Hindu picture of the world.

First we need to resolve the problem of the definition of God, which is not an easy one. It is an enterprise that has already occupied many generations in our own culture and has caused considerable difficulties. However, we may start from the customary view of God in Christian doctrine – and in the broader sense in all the monotheistic religions. Here we see a personified God who has properties: God is omniscient, omnipotent, and utterly good but can also be angry. God loves human beings, his creatures. God is eternal and – a particularly important factor for our further reflections on Hinduism – the creator of heaven and earth. Now this act of creation presupposes particular qualities, and the dilemma for theological thought which arises from this approach has also caused considerable difficulties in the Christian sphere. Who can know how different the course of Christianity might have been had the view of the Syrian Marcion prevailed in the third century, namely that the absolute God can have no properties and therefore cannot be the creator either? Marcion attributed the creation of the world to a 'demiurge'.

Brahman

Brahman (not to be confused with Brahma) is absolute consciousness, the supreme, non-dual reality. It rests in itself, is the Absolute without properties which is unattainable to our senses. Without properties and absolute, Brahman cannot be a creator god either. It is subject and not object, and consequently it cannot be an object of a cult or worship. That is the reason why in the Hindu world one sees virtually no temples to Brahman.

There is no parallel to Brahman in our idea of God, so no comparison is possible.

The 'aspects' of Brahman

As the absoluteness of Brahman must remain inaccessible to human thought, Hindus see certain 'aspects' of this indescribable reality, the gods. So this concept of God has nothing to do with ours: here comparisons must remain superficial and are therefore usually misleading.

Western scholars – and Indian scholars too – have attempted to depict the pantheon of Hindu gods as though Hinduism had originally been a monotheistic religion and only took on polytheistic features at a secondary stage. That is certainly not the case. In the Vedic scriptures, which come from a time when the nomadic peoples from the north immigrated into the Indus valley by Karakorum and the Hindu Kush – in the second millennium before our era – the gods were personified phenomena of nature. The 'Indo-Aryans', as they are usually called, personified the sun, the moon, heaven, the waters, fire and storm. These deities had quite human features, and knew joy and pain, love, sorrow and anger. Their roots go back into prehistoric times, and quite often they recall the Greek pantheon.

As some of these beings reach from Vedic times to the present, they should be mentioned briefly here. Many of the gods who are worshipped in Hindu temples and before domestic altars in every hut today are rooted in them.

Indra embodies power, light and victory. In the mythology of the origin of the world, with his thunderbolt he overcomes the dragon of darkness, frees the dawn from its fetters and has conquered the sun for the world. Many scholars suppose that Indra could be the deification of a historical figure, a tribal leader.

Surya is also a divine being from Vedic times. He goes through the firmament with his sun chariot. But Surya is only one aspect of the sun: Pushan is the light of the solar disc which furthers knowledge and makes spirituality fruitful; Savitri is the life-giving, fertile power of the star.

Agni is a god of fire and bears the sacrifices of human beings into the sphere of the Absolute. He is an age-old god, but has lasted down into the Hindu world of the present. He combines the three levels of the world: heaven, the air – or the 'ether' – and the earth, the dwelling place of human beings. In the Rig Veda, a sacred scripture which was written down somewhere between the twelfth and the eighth centuries before our era, we read the following hymn:

'O Agni, you are the growth of the young shoot, the waters are your seed. Innate in all beings and always growing with them, you bring maturity. The universe lives through you. In the form of the sun, with its rays you take up water from the earth, and then you restore life to all creatures through the showers of rain which you make to flow in their time. All is reborn from you, the plants, the green foliage, the lakes, the healthful pools of water, the whole moist place of Varuna.'

When we read this text, we should remember that it was written down about 3,000 years ago. And presumably it had already been handed down by word of mouth for centuries before this.

Varuna is a deity clothed in a white mantle of light, the preserver of order throughout the cosmos. His name derives from the Sanskrit word vara, 'the wide'. He was probably originally a personification of the all-embracing firmament of heaven, but then underwent a change in significance: today he is a god of the ocean, sea and rivers and as such is depicted by the inflated hood of the cobra.

Rudra seems to be a particularly ancient deity. The name means 'the howling one'. He is a personification of storms, thunder and bad weather, but is sometimes also identified with Agni. Over the course of time Rudra became Bhairava, i.e. Shiva in his 'terrifying form'. Rudra is by no means a being who only brings blessing; he is also thought to bring pestilence to human beings and animals. His sons, the Maruts, are storm gods who ride on the hurricanes.

All these beings who can bring disaster have to be pacified and soothed by sacrifices.

It is difficult to define the deities of this Vedic period; sometimes they cannot even be distinguished from one another. But they show us that moral and ethical notions had been developed even in this early period. However, initially there were as yet no priests, nor any distinct priestly caste. It was for the elders of the tribes to offer the necessary sacrifices. Nor should it be forgotten that the beginnings of its world of ideas coincide with the period when the tribes, which had long been nomads, began to settle in one place. Thus they are part of a social revolution.

In the ancient scriptures we can recognize a marked symbolic element in sacrificial actions. The sacrificial altar, which had to be rebuilt each time, consisted of burnt clay tiles, i.e. earth hardened in the element of fire. The sacrifices were essentially the fruits of the field, and pouring water on them was an essential part of the sacrificial ritual. The elements of fire, water and earth were personified and divinized.

After this excursion into the sphere of the 'dawn' of the Hindu pantheon we must now return to regions whose history can be clearly defined and which are significant for the present. Here, however, we have to make it clear that the present-day world of the Hindu gods is also many centuries old, and it is impossible to recognize a precise transition.

The concept of ishta devata

We have already seen that Brahman, this absolute 'God' without properties resting in itself, cannot be the object of a cult. According to the Hindu view one must turn towards its aspects, its 'reflections' in the relative sphere. This is what the gods are. Before we look more closely at the most important figures from the Hindu pantheon, we must grapple with the concept of the ishta devata.

First let us attempt to get nearer to the concept, which is not easy to approach, by looking at the term. The Sanskrit word ishta means 'beloved', but also 'wish'; devata is most accurately rendered as 'divine essence'. The translation which most correctly renders ishta devata is 'chosen ideal'. Now the sanatana dharma, Hinduism, is largely undogmatic: everyone is free to choose for his or her ishta devata whatever aspect of the Absolute – Brahman – , i.e. the deity, that he finally thinks most necessary for his personal way to redemption, to moksha, to nirvana. The Hindu deities are not in competition with one another, and many people turn to several of these divine aspects, these reflections of Brahman.

As an illustration of this, here is a quotation from an ancient scripture. Vishnu says to Shiva, 'The ignorant think that I am no different from you.'

When I asked a swami, a 'holy' man who lived near the source of the Ganges, about the different gods in the world of Hindu thought, he said: 'They are just names, there is only one God!'

The two quotations cited here put the polytheism of the Hindus which is so often criticized in the West in a different and special light. The cause of the misunderstanding lies simply in the different definitions of God. As I have already said, quite major differences can be noted between the thoughts and knowledge of the spiritual elite and so-called 'popular belief'. But the basic structure is the same for all Hindus. Ordinary people choose their own ishta devata, but then the idea of God becomes independent and often gets suspiciously close to idolatry. It then happens that various village deities, who derive from originally animistic or shamanistic ideas, often come to be worshipped. Furthermore the sacrifice offered to them is also often seen as a *quid pro quo*: the villager sacrifices, and the god fulfils his wishes,

If we want to look more closely at the most important gods of present-day Hindus, we must not lose sight of the concept and content of the ishta devata. Nor should we forget that these divine beings have developed over the course of centuries and that their roots go back deep into prehistoric times.

In Hinduism, not unlike other religions, a trinity of gods has developed, called trimurti. It consists of Brahma (not to be confused with Brahman), Vishnu and Shiva. In accordance with Indian thought, while they differ, they cannot be precisely distinguished from one another. The properties attributed to them in part run parallel and in other respects supplement one another. Vishnu and Shiva with their 'sub-forms' provide by far the most ishta devatas in Hinduism: the Vishnuites are estimated at around seventy per cent and the Shivaites at around twenty-five per cent.

Brahma

In the sphere of Hindu culture there are many very different myths which grapple with the origin of the world. Within the trimurti, Brahma is the absolute deity in his aspect as creator of the world. But like all other gods, he is a notion within the relative sphere, the illusion which Hindus call maya. Brahma is usually depicted with four faces which look to the four points of the compass. In his four hands he holds the four Vedas, the fundamental writings which are the revelations of the sanatana dharma. We shall return to them in discussing scripture and its significance within Hinduism. Here it should already be pointed out in anticipation that in present-day Hinduism, too, these four collections of texts are regarded as unassailable and unchangeable. This is how we are to understand the symbolism of the four Vedas in the hands of the principle of creation. Brahma is celebrated in many hymns, in which he is often called the 'lotus born' and sometimes also 'the one who arose from himself'. The cult of Brahma is much less well represented than worship of Vishnu and Shiva, but in many temples there are chapels with statues which are dedicated to him.

Vishnu

In historical terms, this ishta devata, which is so popular, derives from an age-old sun god; many rites dedicated to him describe his 'three steps': sunrise, the zenith and sunset. The name Vishnu comes from the Sanskrit word vish, which means something like 'effect'. Other mythical figures like Hari and Narayan have been fused with him over the course of the centuries, and today are additional names of his.

Vishnu is understood to be the guardian and preserver of dharma, the eternal law. Whenever this law is in danger of being lost to humankind he appears in this world as an avatar (descent).

In the Hindu understanding the avatars of Vishnu are not born like all other beings through the web of karma but by their own impulse. The followers of Vishnu – called Vishnuites or also Vaishnavas – usually distinguish ten such 'descents' (other schools distinguish twelve); the last – Kalki – will only be born after the end of this world age, the Kali Yuga. Vishnu in the form of his avatar Kalki seems almost like a messiah figure to us Westerners: when this age of Kali Yuga in which we now live one day ends, then Kalki will bring humankind a time of peace, harmony and all misery, and all wretchedness will be forgotten. A world age of inner harmony will dawn.

Here, now, is an attempt at a brief explanation of the avatars, the 'descents' of Vishnu.

Matsya, 'the fish', plays a major role in the Indian saga of the flood, which is clearly older than that in the Gilgamesh epic and in the Bible. Matsya advises Manu, who has caught him as a little fish and at his urgent request has not killed him, to build a ship in order to avoid the coming flood. Manu follows this advice and takes the seven rishis, the teachers of the world, and seeds of all beings of the earth, on board.

Kurma, 'the tortoise', is a mystical object of an age-old legend about the origin of the world. The demons came to 'churn the ocean' – primal matter – in order to steal the drink of immortality hidden on its bed. Vishnu appeared in the form of Kurma, the tortoise, on the bed of the primal ocean to give it firm support. In so doing he got the drink, amrita, and found Lakshmi, the 'Indian Venus', who was born from the ocean and became his consort. (Lakshmi is depicted as a beautiful woman standing on a tortoise.)

Varaha, 'the boar', a further descent of Vishnu, is a mystical figure and the object of a legend which tells how even the gods are in danger and have to defend themselves against beings who have accumulated too much power.

Narasimha, 'the lion man', is a figure in Indian legend who always intervenes when the equilibrium of the world is disturbed by the revolt of humankind against the absoluteness of Brahman. According to the Hindu view, the destruction of this equilibrium within the levels of the universe must lead to the self-destruction of all being.

Vamana, 'the dwarf', in legends fights against and defeats the demon Bali and so saves the world by overcoming the superhuman demon.

Parashurama, 'Rama with the axe', in all probability symbolizes historical events. What we have here is essentially the fight of the priestly caste of Brahmans against the warrior caste of the Kshatriyas for predominance. These struggles over hierarchy certainly played a major role in the history of Hinduism. The caste, which represented the nobility, the generals and the kinds, certainly did not abandon its supremacy to the priestly caste without resistance. In the legends, Parashurama is always depicted as a rough diamond, loveable and fond of life.

The avatars of Vishnu mentioned so far are not really the object of cults, but rather topics of the spiritual speculations of learned Vishnuites. But they are constantly depicted – one example is the sanctuary of Vishnu in Khajraho; little temples are also dedicated to them near to the main sanctuary of Vishnu.

The two 'descents' Rama and Krishna are a very different

matter. For many Hindus they are ishta devatas: personally
chosen aspects of Brahman.

Rama is the great hero of the Ramayana epic. He is the
personification of the fulfilment of duty and moral rigour.
His epic tell us how he – the king – through no fault of his
own loses not only his kingdom but also his beloved spouse
Sita. He has to undergo many hard fights but finally wins
back his kingdom and his wife with the help of the 'monkey
god' Hanuman. Sita had been abducted to Sri Lanka by the
demon king Ravana, but virtuously resisted all his attempts
on her. Once she has returned home to Rama, her husband,
an intrigue begins. Hints are conveyed to the king that his
wife's virtue is not quite so unstained, and that her conduct
towards her abductor had not been so hostile. Rama puts
his beloved Sita before a tribunal. However, she asks
'mother earth' to open and swallow her up to prove her
innocence. This happens, and Rama has to realize that his
doubt and his mistrust at the same time mean his downfall.

The figure of Ravana is significant for Hindu thought. A
highly gifted man misuses his gifts and the powers that he
has acquired in deep meditation. These 'supernatural'
capacities – though the Hindu does not see them in those
terms – are so to speak a by-product of meditation. But they
also represent a danger for those engaged in spiritual
striving who allow themselves to be diverted from their real
way to knowledge. Hindus are convinced that in certain
phases of meditation they can acquire capacities, for
example, to make themselves invisible, to assume other
forms, or even to be present in several places at the same
time. In the eyes of Hindus all this is natural and has
absolutely nothing to do with the 'supernatural'. But these
capacities can be misused and exploited as means of
personal power; they can be 'demonized'. The figure of
Ravana is such a demonic figure, and Rama, a symbol of
spiritual purity, must fight against him.

Krishna is an avatar of Vishnu who is particularly revered in Hinduism. He is the hero of the Bhagavad Gita, one of the best-known writings of Hindu literature. In this epic Krishna teaches Prince Arjuna his obligations before the great decisive battle begins.

The name Krishna is derived from a Sanskrit word which means 'the dark'. The fact that Krishna is usually depicted with a special dark, bluish skin suggests that he is of Dravidian and not of Indo-Aryan origin. This assumption is further supported by the fact that legend assigns him to a geographical area which lies outside the original sphere of the Indo-Aryans.

Krishna is usually depicted as a young man, playing on a flute and surrounded by attractive women. The flute is a symbol which is often used in Indian iconography: it is the human being, who is nothing but a dead thing unless given breath by the deity. At any rate the image of Krishna as a young shepherd, playing with his maidens in a pool decked with lotus flowers – which is far too colourful for our taste – is a portrayal which can often be found in India. One can find such colourful prints everywhere, even in the huts of the poor.

As I have already mentioned, Kalki is the avatar which will appear at the end of the Kali Yuga, the age in which we now live, to reintroduce a Satya Yuga, an age of world harmony.

There are Vishnuite schools which also see a 'descent' of Vishnu in Buddha – and indeed in Jesus. The incorporation of Buddha into the Hindu pantheon is probably to be seen as an act of psychological self-defence: for a long period Buddhism forced back Hinduism in India. A climax of this development was the reign of the emperor Ashoka. But Hindu thought prevailed, and since then Buddhism has no longer had a role in India. So as a kind of gesture Buddha was included in the series of avatars. However, this is not rooted in popular belief.

In present-day Hinduism, Vishnu's 'descents' Rama and Krishna are often fused into an ishta devata; Hindu sects active in Europe and America often begin with Rama Krishna.

Vishnuite thought is especially shaped by the idea of bhakti. By this, Hindus understand something like 'absolute surrender': surrender to the guru but above all to the deity. So bhakti has also been translated 'love of God'. However, in this context too we should not forget that here we have a completely different definition of God from ours.

The portrayal of Vishnu indicates the subordinate role which is assigned to him in the origin of the world: he is usually shown resting on a 'world serpent' in a pool. One good example of this is Anata Shayin Narayan (these are all names of Vishnu) not far from the village of Buddhanilkanta in Nepal. The deity rests on the great world serpent, whose five heads protect his own. This portrayal dates from the seventh century and is still visited by many pilgrims today. The pool in which the statue lies represents the primal sea, the 'ocean' of the old legends – we would call it primal matter. The king of Nepal, who by legend was an incarnation of Vishnu, might never look at this statue – which was himself; the belief of these people was that if he did he would immediately leave this earthly life.

We meet adherents of Vishnu all over India: they can be recognized by the vertical stripes on their foreheads. Many Vishnuite pilgrims go up to one of their holy places, Badrinath. This place is about ten thousand feet above sea level on the Alaknanda, one of the two sources of the Ganges in the Himalayas. A statue of black stone in the temple of Badrinath is an object of particular devotion. It is Vishnu in his form as Narayan. Legend reports that the holy statue was found on the bed of the Alaknanda by an ardent worshipper of Vishnu and brought to the temple. However, it seems originally to have been a depiction of Buddha which then – when Hinduism again triumphed in this area – was given a different function.

Another place which is particularly important to Vishnuites is in Puri in the Indian union state of Orissa. A great waggon festival takes place there every year in which Vishnu is led through the city on his giant processional waggon in his form as Jagannath (Vishnu-Krishna). This word is the origin of our term 'juggernaut'. Time and again believers are crushed by the gigantic wooden wheels of this waggon, and it is hard to tell whether these are accidents or ecstatic suicides. However, Hinduism condemns suicide on principle: it represents violent intervention in the existing web of karma. Those who commit suicide 'so to speak get in the way of the karma assigned to them'.

Those who are not Hindus may not enter the Jagannath sanctuary in Puri. An Englishman dressed as a Hindu is said to have paid for his attempt with his life.

In Vishnuism, in contrast to Shivaism, the female extension to the deity, his shakti, plays a subordinate role. Certainly Lakshmi, the consort of Vishnu, whom he won when he prevented the 'churning of the ocean', primal matter, is worshipped and depicted in pictures, but she has very little significance in cultic actions. She is regarded as an embodiment of beauty and feminine charm.

To sum up what has been said about Vishnu and his followers, the Vishnuites: Vishnu is a figure from the Hindu pantheon who – in contrast to Shiva – is always thought of as being concerned for humankind and is also gentle. Vishnu always appears as a helper of humankind when the 'eternal law' is in danger of being lost, in the form of an avatar, a 'descent' to earth. The ideal of the Vishnuites is bhakti, dedication to the deity but also – in an extended sense – to fellow men and women, to crea-

tion. Vishnu and especially his 'descents' Rama and Krishna
are the most frequent ishta devatas in modern Hinduism.

Shiva

Shiva, the third figure of the trimurti, the 'divine trinity' in
Hinduism, is an ambivalent figure which we find difficult to
grasp, a being who combines very different properties. He is
the bringer of blessing and also the destroyer of the
imaginary world of appearances. This last property, of
destroyer, is not surprising: Hindus always see all processes
within the world that can be perceived by the human senses
as cycles. So Shiva destroys in order to build up, in order to
maintain the cycle of all being between becoming and
passing away. As the embodiment of the 'supreme reality'
he destroys human rootedness in an imaginary, untrue,
deceptive world of the senses which stands in the way of the
knowledge of the Absolute, the attainment of moksha.

Shiva often has a crescent moon in his hair, a symbol
which associates him with the cycles of months. The third
eye on his forehead is explained to us by an age-old legend:
once Parvati – Shiva's consort – closed his eyes in love play.
Then this third, mystical, all-knowing eye formed on his
forehead. This eye on the forehead is an attribute which can
be found frequently, and not just in Hindu mythology. It is
thought of as the instrument of the 'other seeing', spiritual
vision. The two 'normal eyes' can perceive only optical
impressions which – if we follow Indian thinking – have an
illusory character.

It should be pointed out in passing that the 'spiritual eye'
regularly plays a significant role in other cultures as well.
We need only think of the representation of the Holy Spirit
as an eye in a triangle. Moreover the story of a sense-organ
like an eye which human beings have lost in the course of
their development has constantly haunted people. Thus it is

also claimed that the human pineal gland is a rudimentary 'survival' of this organ.

Shiva is a figure who with a degree of probability verging on certainty originally had his home in the region of the Himalayas. Legend sees him enthroned on Kailash, a mountain in Tibet almost 20,000 feet high, which is reflected in Lake Manasarovar, the 'Lake of Mental Thought'. This ice-covered mountain, which towers from the chain of the Himalayas like a bastion in the high plateau of Tibet, is sacred not only to Hindus but to Buddhists. Members of both religions undertake the difficult pilgrimage to it and make a ritual circuit of Kailash.

A further legend about Shiva tells us that he once saved humankind. The gods resolved to direct the Milky Way to earth and form the sacred river Ganges from it. The masses of water which now hurtled down from heaven would have annihilated humankind, had not Shiva caught them in the knots of his hair and thus diminished their destructive force. We can see in this legend a variant of the flood saga, which is evidently known to all cultures.

Like other gods, Shiva, too, is endowed with a whole saga of symbols and mystical attributes. The crescent moon in his hair has already been mentioned. It is not only a reference to his connection with the cycles of the months, but also a symbol of the cyclical course of nature, and indeed of world history. Shiva's mysterious mount is the white bull, certainly an age-old fertility symbol. This bull, named Nandi, often stands for the mystical presence of Shiva. We see it in front of or also in temples dedicated to him. Sometimes Shiva is depicted with many arms and clad in a tiger skin. He then holds in his four, eight or sixteen hands objects including an arrow, a drum, a club, a noose and the trishula (trident). We also keep seeing this attribute on the pilgrim routes to sanctuaries of Shiva. The Shivaites or Shaivites, as the adherents of this popular ishta devata call themselves, can be recognized by the horizontal stripes on their foreheads. They often carry on their pilgrimages a staff with the trident of Shiva, the trishula, and always ram it into the ground where they want to stay.

Shiva – himself an aspect of the absolute of Brahman – in turn has many aspects and names which have been bestowed on him by Hindu piety over the course of centuries. Here, briefly, are the most important of them.

In the West, depictions of Shiva as Nataraja ('king of the dance') are the best known. Such statues can be found in any Indian souvenir shop and are coveted souvenirs for those who go to India. Nataraja symbolizes the cosmic dance and represents its five activities: creation, preservation, destruction, embodiment and liberation. One foot of the dancing Shiva crushes the demon of not-knowing; the other – raised high – symbolizes the state beyond consciousness. The garland of flames which surrounds Nataraja is seen as the dance of natural forces. The ecstatic-cosmic dance of the worlds could be defined – in our thought categories – as the 'inexorable dance of evolution'.

As Pashupati, Shiva is the 'lord of wild animals'. This form of Shiva is particularly worshipped for example at a temple complex – Pashupatinath – in Kathmandu in Nepal.

Another aspect of Shiva is Mahayogin ('the great yogin'). As such he is the lord of itinerant ascetics and the yogins, i.e. those who seek their way to knowledge on the various stages of Yoga. Shiva as Mahayogin is an ascetic figure usually smeared with ash and naked.

There are also depictions of Shiva which show him as half-man, half-woman. He is then Aradhanareshvara, in whom duality is transcended. He has become a unity with his shakti, just as the absolute truth knows no polarity and issues in the 'all-one'.

Shiva is alleged to have 1,008 names and aspects. Hindus can see unity in this multiplicity which is so confusing for us. Thus for example Shiva is also Vishesvara, 'Lord of the Universe'. In this form he also embodies creation, preservation, destruction and liberation from not-knowing, in a completely analogous way to the symbolism of the cosmic dance, the Nataraja.

To give a reasonably comprehensive description of the nature of Shiva, I must here anticipate and refer to things which will be illustrated more clearly when we come to discuss Tantrism. The dual view which is dominant in Hinduism and especially in Shivaism leads to two views: first, every male deity has a female counterpart who is called shakti. Secondly, any divine being has two opposing aspects, one 'peaceful' and the other 'terrifying'. In Indian thought this dualistic view of the world expresses the knowledge that there is polarity, opposition, in the relative, non-absolute sphere which is accessible to our senses. (Similar considerations also underlie particular schools of Buddhism.)

Now back to the figure of Shiva. I have already mentioned that as Aradhanareshvana he transcends the polarity of the sexes in himself. In this connection it may be interesting that depictions of Shiva very often have a special feature: in one ear he wears an ornament of the kind that men wear, and in the other one characteristic of a woman. In addition Shiva has several female counterparts (shaktis). We have already met one of them in the figure of Parvati. Her name also denotes her origin: Parvati means 'belonging to the mountains'. Thus she comes – like Shiva himself – from the Himalayas ('the land of the snows') and is also enthroned with her consort on the summit of Kailash. According to another legend Shiva is Sankara and Parvati his shakti Gauri. The two are enthroned on a summit in the Everest group – which is called Gauri Sankar. Nor is it surprising

that Shiva and Parvati – notions which arose in the
countries of the Himalayas – underwent many changes and
extensions on their way to South India and into other
regions of southern and Eastern Asia.

Only two of the many shaktis of Shiva need to be
mentioned here.

Durga ('the unfathomable') is an ambiguous being,
sometimes terrifying, and sometimes bringing help and
blessing. She fights against and destroys the demon of not-
knowing which is governed by karma, and supports all
those who strive for the realization of God. Among the
many functions attributed to her by popular belief, one
should be mentioned here. In the great temple of Durga in
Calcutta women pray for children, and especially of course
for sons. Time and again they lay their sacrifice on the
symbols of Durga adorned with hibiscus blossoms: the
sacrificial priests of the temple clearly do not go short. If
their ardent prayer is successful, the women bring their sons
to the temple to show them to the deity and to thank her.
And perhaps also to ask for the blessing of further children.

Kali ('the black one') as Shiva's shakti is a terrifying being
who is also worshipped as 'divine mother'. In accordance
with Tantric notions Kali is often depicted in sexual union
with Shiva: he then symbolizes the transcendent aspect, the
primal force.

Kali and Durga often coalesce and then as Kali Durga are
identified with Bhairavi, the 'terrifying one'. The pujas
(ritual sacrificial actions) for this female, terrifying dual
goddess often last for days and are accompanied by the
sacrifice of animals. The animals – usually goats, sheep or
chickens – have their carotid arteries severed in a flash by
the sacrificial priest and the blood sprays over the statue of
the goddess, which quickly becomes a now unrecognizable
mass of congealed blood. Such animal sacrifices seem to be
in blatant contradiction to the Hindu prohibition against

killing. However – as in many other cases – we must simply note that our Western logic is not always the 'key to the castle'.

Shiva himself also has a terrifying aspect: it is Bhairava, a name which is derived from a Sanskrit word meaning 'terrifying', the terrible. This form of Shiva, too, is an object of worship; a larger-than-life portrait in the middle of the city of Kathmandu is an example of it. Every day, many believers gather before the larger-than-life bas-relief to offer their devotion and set down their small sacrifices.

One special feature of Shivaism is the lingam-yoni symbolism, which has its spiritual roots in Tantric thinking, the notion of the dualism of being as experienced in relativity. The lingam (or linga) is a stone pillar or a cone made of some other material and represents the phallus, the male member. A lingam pillar also has on it faces of Shiva facing the four points of the compass. So the lingam is a symbol of Shiva. This seems remarkable to us, since here the mystical destroyer is being personified by a fertility symbol. Yoni is the symbol of the female sexual organ and is either round or, more usually, depicted by a triangle on its apex. Shiva's lingam is placed in Parvati's yoni, thus depicting dualism pictorially. But it would be quite wrong to see this world of symbols, which is so alien to us, only as sexual exhibition. To Indians, who have a quite different attitude to sexuality from us, such an interpretation seems completely wrong. One finds the lingam-yoni symbols everywhere, in the temples, on the streets, by public wells and so on. Time and again one can see pious people decorating the lingam with flowers and pouring an offering of water over the symbolic depiction. The combination of the lingam with the yoni often appears in the holy of holies in the temples and thus indicates the presence of the deities.

Shiva and his shakti Parvati are an exceptionally popular divine couple. So inevitably a son has been given to them, so that they become a divine family. This is Ganesha, the deity with the elephant head. He, too, enjoys great popularity as the one who prepares the way and brings good fortune, the god on whom one calls in order to avoid difficulty. But why do Hindus see this deity as having an elephant head? Here legend tells us that Parvati, the young mother, proudly showed her new-born son around – as young mothers do – seeking admiration for her handsome child. She also did this to the planetary god Shani, completely forgetting that everything that this god looks upon immediately turns to ashes. Deeply terrified, Parvati turned to Brahma for help. He advised putting on the child the head of the first being she encountered. It was an elephant . . . What is unique and inexplicable is why Ganesha is always depicted with only one tusk; the second is broken off.

Shiva and his shaktis, his female counterparts, and Ganesha, the one with an elephant head, together form a divine family which is exceptionally alive and popular in Indian Hinduism. Time and again we shall find pictures or sculptures of these beings, and here deep spirituality and profanity can lie side by side. Thus for example those who offer sacrifice leave the temple of Durga, reeking with blood, to have a happy picnic somewhere in its shade; or we see attractive pictures of the deities on the windscreens of overloaded buses and trucks, or we are struck by the fact that at the ghats in Varanasi (Benares) which are held to be so sacred, above the burning places, next to a gigantic picture of Shiva there is an equally large advertisement for a Japanese electronics firm. Hindus see no contradiction here: it is all part of the phenomenon of earthly life.

A ghat is a terraced area leading down to water which is regarded as sacred. The buildings which go with this are also called ghats in the wider sense.

In Shivaism, Shaktism, the notion of the supplementation of a male deity with a female entity, is very marked.

Here is a brief summary of what has been said about Shiva.

Shiva is a very complex figure of the Hindu pantheon who has a great variety of often apparently contradictory properties. While he is involved in the creation of the worlds, he acts as destroyer, in order to keep the eternal cycles of history in motion. As Nataraja he dances the inexorable dance of evolution; he destroys the demon of not-knowing. Shiva has a series of aspects, and his cult puts special emphasis on the dualistic idea of all being; quite a large part of the doctrine of the Shivaites has a clearly Tantric colouring.

Other gods in the Hindu pantheon

Though the number of deities worshipped in Hinduism seems to us Westerners to be infinitely great, it is the beings of the trimurti with their feminine counterparts, the shaktis, who are understood as ishta devatas by the vast majority of Hindus. So here I shall only describe briefly a few other deities whom travellers to India will encounter here and there. However, it is important to note that for Hindus the worship of one god in no way excludes the worship of another. The Hindu gods do not seem to be jealous of one another.

We have already made the acquaintance of Hanuman (also Hanumat) as Rama's helper in his battle against the demon king Ravana in the Ramayana epic. His adventure is described in the Hanuman Nataka, the 'Great Drama of Hanuman', in lively scenes in which supernatural powers are attributed to the monkey-like figure. He can fly, he moves trees and mountains, and directs the clouds. However, for Hindus he is also the embodiment and symbol of an obedient attitude to his master, a virtue which is to be attributed to the bhakti, the love of God in Vishnuism. This and his role in the Ramayana make Hanuman really seem to belong to the spiritual world of the Vishnuites.

It has been asked time and again what the monkey form of Hanuman really means. One attempt at an explanation derives his form from a military standard. At any rate it is a fact that armies of the Rajahs, the princes, used standards with animal emblems at a very early stage. So it may be that the figure of Hanuman ultimately owes its origin to the fantastic divinization of a historical figure, a hero of the early period.

Hanuman is very popular in present-day Hinduism, and his statues are often smeared with a red paste to the point of becoming unrecognizable (one example is the statue at the Hanuman gate of the Old Palace in Katmandu).

Those travelling to India can also find the monkey figure of Hanuman elsewhere: people dress up as monkeys with long tails and beg from pilgrims – and of course also from foreigners – with strange hissing sounds.

The 'great drama of Hanuman' is sometimes staged in all its fourteen acts and arouses great enthusiasm among the audience.

Vishvakarma, a deity who is certainly very old, has undergone a remarkable change of significance in the course of time. The name comes from the Sanskrit and means 'active everywhere', 'all-creative'. In the Rig Veda, probably the oldest scripture that has come down to us and the first Veda, Vishvakarma is regarded as the personification of all-embracing creative activity. In the course of the centuries he became the guardian deity of smiths. But in present-day Hinduism he has become a real 'patron of the workers' and has an annual feast. I had the opportunity of taking part in this feast at Triveni Ghat in Rishikesh on the upper reaches of the Ganges. Young workers brought his statue, decorated with flowers, on a truck to the bank of the Ganges and there immersed it in the holy water. The truck with the statue went in the midst of a procession at walking pace, accompanied by trumpets and drums, which made a noisy spectacle to which hymns and songs through a crackling loudspeaker made an appropriate contribution. All in all this was markedly a festival of joy and relaxation.

The name Hari – freely translated 'the one who drives away sin' – is often used as an extra name for Vishnu or one of his avatars, but it also denotes any other ishta devata, an aspect of the deity chosen personally. Hari is also used as a mantra, as a mystical syllable to which a spiritual power is attributed. Hence, too, the repetition of Hari Om as a litany in ritual actions.

Hara is a form of address to Shiva which is often used. The Hindus have now formed a kind of 'one god', Harihara, from the two.

Legend tells us the following story in this connection. One day his god appeared to a Vishnuite with two faces, as Vishnu and Shiva at the same time. In accordance with his tradition the Vishnuite sacrificed only to 'his' god, but the sacrifice was brusquely rejected. The pious man had to learn that ultimately there can only be 'one all'.

This legend shows us the view of the spiritually advanced Hindu, but it should be pointed out that such considerations are almost completely absent from popular belief.

Alongside the divine beings described here, Hinduism knows many others, which are partly aspects of the 'main deities' and partly so-called 'lower' beings or demons. The latter in particular are thought of as mortal. The length of their lives is a 'world period', i.e. 311,040 billion human years. (We shall be going into the mythical calculation of time underlying this figure in due course.)

The countless gods of Hinduism are aspects, reflections, emanations of absoluteness, of Brahman. Only as such are they comprehensible to human beings and can they become the objects of cults. Western scholars have divided the complicated pantheon into classes of gods, families of gods. The trimurti, the divine trinity in Hinduism, brings together three aspects of Brahman, the Absolute which is not accessible to humankind: Brahma, the creator; Vishnu, the sustainer; and Shiva, the destroyer, who keeps the wheel of the cyclical courses of world history in motion. The properties assigned to the three divine beings overlap and supplement one another. According to Hindu understanding, the absolute God Brahman, without properties and resting in itself, cannot be a conversation partner for human beings. Hence the notion of the ishta devata, the 'personally chosen' aspect of Brahman, the Absolute which cannot be grasped.

4

The Hindu Scriptures

Hinduism is not a religion with a founder; it has no historical personality like Moses, Jesus, Muhammad or Buddha. However, Hinduism is very much a religion of revelation. The four Vedas – and also other writings – claim to have been revealed. Legend tells us that in the dawn of prehistory there were seven rishis – 'teachers of humankind' – who received the revelation of the Vedas; it even gives their names, but these cannot be verified historically. They are also called Brahma-rishis, proclaimers of the divine and earthly order.

We Westerners should remember that an exact historiography, an absolute historical consciousness which is orientated on a specific point in time – whether the birth of Christ or the hijra of Muhammad – appears only relatively late in human history and thus represents a kind of new cultural attainment. But we would do well not to underestimate the preciseness of oral tradition. The handing down of texts by word of mouth was once of unprecedented importance. In the course of this discussion of the canonical scriptures of Hinduism we shall discover that handing them down word for word – with a precision extending even to emphasis – was regarded as vitally important. This is not least the reason for the rise of a hereditary and powerful priestly caste, the Brahmans, in Hinduism. In other cultural circles, too, it can be demonstrated that oral tradition is quite surprisingly accurate and reliable.

Before we concern ourselves in more detail with the canonical scriptures, we should at least touch on the 'chronology' used in the Hindu world-view.

Hindus speak of a kalpa, by which they understand 'a day and a night of Brahma'. A kalpa lasts 12,000 divine years, which corresponds to 4,320,000 human years. One hundred Brahma years are 31,040 billion (!) human years. Four periods keep alternating within this framework of time:

Satya Yuga	1,728,000 human years
Treta Yuyga	1,296,000 human years
Dwapara Yuga	864,000 human years
Kali Yuga	432,000 human years.

We now live in the Kali Yuga, the 'blackest' period, which in the view of Hindus began with the death of Krishna in the year 3102 before our reckoning. At the end of this age Kalki, the 'descent' of Vishnu on earth, will appear and usher in a new Satya Yuga, an age of peace and harmony.

This excursion into Hindu ideas of time should make clear to us the chronological presuppositions underlying Indian philosophy.

However, it should be pointed out here that there are Hindu philosophers who derive the calculation based on such gigantic figures from a 'translation mistake' in the age-old Sanskrit texts of the Rig Veda.

The four Vedas

For the orthodox Hindu, these scriptures are of superhuman origin and have divine authority. Together they are six times as long as the Christian Bible and for the most part were written in an archaic Sanskrit. This poses a not inconsiderable difficulty, since some passages can hardly be translated and therefore have been interpreted in different ways.

The four Vedas (Veda is to be translated 'knowledge', 'sacred teaching') are:

Rig Veda   Veda of the Verses
Sama Veda   Veda of the Songs
Yajur Veda   Veda of the sacrificial sayings
Atharva Veda Veda of Atharvan (a mystical fire priest)

Each of these writings has been subdivided by content (collection, explanation of ritual, etc.); in addition, a 'work part' and a 'knowledge part' have also been distinguished.

The Rig Veda

Veda means 'sacred knowledge', and Rig has been reasonably correctly translated 'verse'. It is generally agreed that this scripture, which contains ten 'cycles of songs' consisting of a total of 1,028 hymns with 10,580 verses, was written down between the twelfth and eighth centuries before our era. The oral tradition certainly goes back much further. The 'song cycles' of the Rig Veda are named after the rishis to whom according to legend the texts were revealed.

To give a brief indication of the pattern of thought in the Rig Veda, here is part of a hymn about the origin of the world:

'Then was not existent nor existent: there was no realm of air, no sky beyond it.
   What covered in, and where? And what gave shelter? Was water there, unfathomed depth of water?

Death was not then, nor was there anything immortal: no sign was there, the day's and night's divider.

That one thing, breathless, breathed by its own nature: apart from it was nothing whatsoever.

Darkness there was: at first concealed in darkness, this all was undiscriminated chaos.

All that existed then was void and formless: by the great power of warmth was born that unit.

Thereafter rose desire in the beginning, desire, the primal seed and germ of spirit.

Sages who searched with their heart's thought discovered the existent's kinship in the non-existent . . .

Who truly knows and who can here declare it, whence it was born and whence came this creation?

The gods are later than this world's production. Who knows, then, whence it first came into being?

He, the first origin of this creation, whether he formed it all or did not form it,

Whose eye controls this world in highest heaven, he truly knows it, or perhaps he knows not.'

This brief extract from the Rig Veda illustrates for us the thinking of people who lived and thought thousands of years ago. Here we must also take into account that any translation – even the best – detracts from the substance of a statement. Moreover, many texts in Indian literature are of an apocryphal kind; they are ambiguous or can be interpreted in many ways, and the initiated detect different meanings in them from the laity, the uninitiated.

Another text from the Rig Veda is about burying the ashes of a dead person and gives us some insight into the ritual for the dead in this distant period.

'Slip down in the mother, in this earth, the broad, spacious earth, the kindly earth.

Soft as wool, as a young woman for the one who has acted piously, shall she protect you from the womb of annihilation.

Open, O earth, oppress him not, receive him graciously, take him gently in your embrace, cover him, O earth, as a mother covers her child with the end of her garment!

May the earth which opens up hold fast, and thousands of posts rise up from it; may this abode drip with butter and be a refuge to him for all times.

I pile up the earth around you, setting down this sod, that no harm may come to me. May these pillars hold the fathers to you, Yama, and prepare an abode for you here.'

This hymn from the Rig Veda cites the proclamation of the sacrificing priest in connection with the burial of the ashes of a dead person. (Yama is a god of the dead, a ruler of the realm of the dead, who is often understood as the judge of the dead.)

This text shows us much human warmth, but also the manifestly age-old human anxiety that the dead might return and do harm to the living.

The Sama Veda

The Sama Veda, the 'Veda of songs', takes up the Rig Veda in content and sets its verses and strophes to music, i.e. provides them with notation. Many of these prayers, which are sung as folk songs, are still alive today, though their ancient Sanskrit is now hardly comprehensible.

Originally the udgatri (singer) sang from this collection of songs. He is one of the four chief priests in the ritual of the soma offering. (Soma is an intoxicating drink made by strictly secret recipes from creepers and only drunk by the sacrificing priests on very special occasions.)

The Sama Veda consists of 1,559 verses, of which only 78 cannot be derived from the Rig Veda.

The Yajur Veda

A distinction is made between the archaic 'Black Yajur Veda' which was composed about 1000 years before our era, and the later 'White Yajur Veda', which is also called the 'Ordered' Veda.

The Yajur Veda contains not only a collection of sayings for sacrifices, mystical mantras and liturgical regulations, but also very precise medical treatments. Here is a text about assuaging Rudra:

'All honour, Rudra, to your wrath and all honour to your arrow; honour to your bow and honour to your arms. May your friendly countenance, O Rudra, look upon us graciously, O dweller in the mountains, and not that countenance which is dark and terrible. Make gracious, O mountain-dweller, the arrow that you hold in your hand to shoot; may it kill neither man nor living being! With saving words we call on you, O dweller in the mountains, to be gracious to all our people when you encounter them.

The intercessor, the first physician of the gods, has spoken for us: trample on all serpents, and drive away the demons. We turn away the wrath of the bringer of salvation, the copper-coloured, reddish-brown one, and those Rudras who live by the thousands in all directions.

The one in red with the blue neck has crept down and the shepherds have seen him, and those women who carry water. May he be gracious to us, and all beings who have been seen there. I have offered worship to the one with the dark hair and the thousand eyes, the generous one, and I have also offered worship to the hosts of his warriors.'

Such ritual texts were vitally important for people. In their way of thinking, society depended for good or ill on the correct recitation of them.

Here is one of the many strophes of another hymn from the Yajur Veda:

'May the divine thought which roams afar when one is awake and returns when one is asleep, the only light of lights, which wanders afar, help my thought to a good decision.'

Each of these strophes, which go on to speak of human knowledge, consciousness and inner will, ends with this stereotyped litany: 'help my thought to a good decision.' We can imagine that this form of recitation made a deep impact on its hearers. The term 'decision' could be translated in modern language as 'motivation'.

The collections of the Yajur Veda come for the most part from a period when the Indo-Aryans had already penetrated into the Punjab and the valley of the Ganges.

The Atharva Veda

The Atharva Veda is also called the 'Veda of Magical Sayings'. It is certainly the latest of the four Vedic scriptures and is hard to demarcate from other scriptures. Many of the texts have an apocryphal character and some are also textbooks of later schools of Hinduism. The Atharva Veda has preserved a whole series of ceremonies which are to be attributed to popular belief: ceremonies of expiation, curses, marriage and funeral songs, and so on. But medical topics are also discussed, sometimes at great length. As an example, here is a spell against fever:

'May Agni drive the fever from here and the pestle, and varuna which have real power, and the places of sacrifice, the straw of the sacrifice, the flaming hearths – away with the fiend!

You who make all things yellow, you who make things glow like Agni, you who bring tremblings, demon of fever, now may you be powerless! Depart, descend, away with you!

Drive away the knotty fever, that produces knots, that is like red dust, you who have power! Drive the fever away now that I have bowed down before it.

O fever, with your brother, consumption, and your sister, the cough, with your cousin, scabies, go away to that people!

Drive away the three-day fever, the fever which lasts for more than three days, the chronic fever and the autumn fever, the cold fever, the hot fever, the summer fever and the fever that comes with the rains!'

It may almost cheer us that here we are confronted with a principle which has evidently survived over the millennia: the fever is quite simply wished on other people! Here is an old Indian variant of the principle of St Florian.

The description of the symptoms and the different kinds of fever is very interesting. A doctor today can easily have some idea of the forms of illness described.

Here is a brief summary of what has been said about the Vedas. They are scriptures which go back to the millennia before our era; at first they were handed down orally according to strict rules and then they were written down. Present-day Hinduism also regards the four Vedas as canonical writings from which recitations are made for various ceremonies and solemn sacrificial actions. However, they are composed in a very archaic Sanskrit which today only a few Brahmans can understand. In addition to their religious, spiritual character, the Vedic scriptures offer us a very vivid picture of the thoughts and feelings of people thousands of years ago.

Sruti and smriti

Hindu philosophical and religious literature distinguishes two terms:

Sruti are writings which have absolutely binding, canonical character. These include the Vedas, whose 'eternal sacred sound' was heard by the rishis, the teachers of humankind; the Samhitas, i.e. songs and sacrificial sayings from the Vedas collected and arranged in various writings; the Brahmanas – each Veda has a Brahmana, an introduction with explanations; and the Upanishads, which are so to speak the concluding part of the sruti. Some Hindu schools also include certain sutras – summaries from the Brahmanas in short, easily understandable statements – among the sruti.

The smriti are similarly holy scriptures, but they have canonical character only when they relate directly to a sruti.

This is not the place to concern ourselves at length with any of these works; we must limit ourselves to those statements which are particularly decisive and characteristic of Hindu thought.

One could describe the Brahmanas as it were as the works of orthodoxy within the Vedic model of thought. They escape any attempt at exact dating and in all probability were written down over a very long period. Some have a markedly formal character, and give the impression that here as it were a compact is being made. The person sacrifices to the deity and then presupposes that a quid pro quo will be given in the form of the fulfilment of his wishes. We cannot avoid the impression that the philosophy underlying the Brahmanas is very remote from the thought of the Vedic scriptures.

I have already pointed out that the Upanishads are counted among the sruti, the canonical binding scriptures. I would like to look rather more closely at these, since they are of quite special importance for Hindu thought – in the present as well.

First of all an explanation of the word Upanishad. 'Upa' means 'near to you', 'ni' means 'down' and 'shad' means 'sit'. So freely translated, the term means 'sit next to someone'. It refers to sitting at the feet of the guru to receive confidential, secret teaching. As I have already explained, the Upanishads form the conclusion of the sruti and are the essential basis of the Vedanta, the philosophical conclusions from the Vedas.

The Upanishads are writings which contain the most profound philosophical and metaphysical insights. Before we go into them more closely we must grapple with yet another term, atman.

We have heard that in Hinduism Brahman is the Absolute without properties which rests in itself. To put it simply, the following notion underlies atman. There is a particle of this Brahman, this Absolute, in every being, in every person. This 'particle', atman, is eternal, indestructible and subject neither to death nor to corruption. One might be inclined to compare it with our concept of the soul, but there is a quite decisive difference: atman is not personal, and whereas our soul goes to God after death, atman when detached from the person returns to the infinite reservoir of the Absolute. Here is a section from the Kathaka Upanishad (1.20–23):

> 'Smaller than the smallest, greater than the greatest, arman rests in the hearts of creatures. The glory of atman is seen by the one who has no desires, no concerns, as a result of the grace of the creator. It sits and yet travels afar; it lies and yet goes everywhere. The one who has recognized the great, all-pervasive atman, the incorporeal in the corporeal, the constant in the inconstant, no longer feels pain. This atman cannot be attained by teaching, nor though understanding, nor through much learning. It is to be attained through the one who chooses this atman; to him this atman discloses its form.'

This strophe from the Upanishads teaches us how decisive the guru, the spiritual teacher, is. Only he can provide atman with a form again for his pupils in their spiritual striving.

In the Mandukya Upanishad atman is compared with the spark of a fire.

> 'Just as thousands of sparks fly from one blazing fire, all of the same kind, so, my friend. manifold being is produced from the imperishable and returns to it again.'

This concept of atman in the Upanishads is not easy for the non-Hindu to understand, but for the Hindu it is a constant in the search for spiritual truth. A fable which is certainly very old may illustrate this:

> Svetaketu wanted to know from his father what atman, this particle of Brahman, really is. 'Throw this salt into

water,' commanded his aged father. Svetaketu did so. 'Bring me the salt that you threw into the water yesterday,' his father asked him the next day. But the son could not find it, because it had disappeared. 'Take a sip from the surface of the water. How does it taste?' 'It's salty.' Take a sip from the middle. What's it like?' 'It's salty, father.' 'Take another sip from the bottom. How does it taste?' 'The same, father.' 'Pour the water out and come with me,' said his father. 'Here truly, my son, you do not grasp being, yet it is here. What is the finest and most fleeting is the true reality. That is atman, and that is what you are.'

This 'that is what you are', 'tat tvam asi', is one of the key statements of the Upanishads.

The analysis of consciousness and knowledge is a special theme of these writings. However, it is also unmistakably stated that Brahman, the Absolute – and thus also atman – remains unattainable to human understanding. But the human longing to come nearer to Brahman beyond these limits of understanding is ultimately our mission. So the Upanishads postulate a deep longing for God. Although they depend heavily on the Vedic scriptures, their powerful freedom of thought and their extension towards transcendence makes them particularly valuable for those in search of the truth.

Brief mention should also be made here of the Vedanta. Veda, as we saw, means knowledge, and anta is to be translated 'conclusion', 'end'. What is meant is that the Vedanta are to be regarded as concluding reflections on the Vedas. Radhakrishnan, one of the great Hindu philosophers of our century, wrote in his book *Indian Philosophy* (which appeared in 1955): 'Of all the Hindu thought systems, Vedanta philosophy is most closely linked to Indian religion and in one form or another influences the world view of every Hindu thinker of the present day.' The Vedanta is concerned in depth with Brahman and atman and the relationship between the two. But special emphasis is constantly placed on the authority of the Vedas.

The Puranas are among the writings to be classed as smriti. The theme of the Puranas is creation, destruction and new creation; they depict the 'sequence of generations' of the gods, the heroes and the manus. (A manu is a mythical being which represents as it were an intermediate stage between gods and human beings, an evolutionary element in the formation of the human race.)

The Puranas put the virtue of bhakti, the love of God, quite specially in the foreground and therefore are particularly important for the adherents of Vishnu. Here is a free rendering of a story which may clarify the thought world of the Puranas:

A virtuous king, who had achieved much karmic merit, was taken by the servants of Yama, the guardian of the realm of the dead, to the underworld, to 'hell'. He refused to return to the world because of the wretchedness of the damned. Now the narrator depicts the cry of those in pain: 'Grant us this grace, o king, remain for a moment, for the air which touches your limbs strengthens our hearts and diminishes the pressure of our suffering.' The king, filled with the deepest compassion, steadfastly refuses to leave the fearful place: 'It seems to me that not once in the world of Brahmans does a person have such good fortune as this, when one can bring relief to suffering creatures. If my presence makes them suffer less, I will not go, but will remain here steadfast as a mountain.' Yama and the other gods try to persuade him to change his mind, but he refuses: 'How will human beings attain what they wish if they are not allowed to turn to my presence. Lord of the two and thirty gods,

release these sinners condemned to torment for the sake
of my good deeds.' Then Indra says, 'You have attained
the highest level. Behold these sinners; for your sake they
are free.'

At first we might think that this is a servile hymn of praise to
a powerful ruler, but that is not the case. The term 'king'
does not refer here to the representative of a power, but
denotes a man depicted here in allegorical terms who by
assimilating his karma to the Absolute has attained 'spiritual power'. Here too an important aspect of bhakti thought
is particularly clear: bhakti is in no way just love of God, but
compassion and concern for fellow human beings, fellow-
creatures, for these have atman, the 'particle' of the
Absolute, in them.

The Tantras also belong to the non-canonical writings,
the smritis. The topic of these writings is the divine creative
power and energy, properties which are identified with the
shakti, the female principle, in dualism, and are personified
as devi, as a goddess. Polarity is also a determinative
element within the Tantric system of thought: each of these
devis is thought of in a gracious and a terrifying form.

This Tantric Shaktism – the word devi is essentially to be
identified with shakti – appears in various trends of Hindu
religion, and also in certain schools of Buddhism. We have
already come to see its role in Shivaism.

Two schools are distinguished in Tantrism: the right-
hand way attaches value to the strictest discipline, and the
left-hand way to unbridled, orgiastic excesses, especially in
the sexual sphere. However, one principle is common to
both schools: absolute dedication to the 'divine mother'.

We can begin from the fact that Tantrism is one of the
many Indian spiritual schools. If we leave aside the sexual
excesses engaged in in its name, which doubtless occur, it is
a philosophical system which needs to be taken seriously. It

may be that ancient matriarchal ideas live on in the worship of the 'divine mother'.

In the sphere of Tantrism one is constantly faced with images or sculptures which depict the divine properties – we might remember in this context that the Hindu definition of God is quite different from ours – in yab-yum (sexual union: yab-yum means 'father-mother'). Anyone who thinks that this is blasphemous should remember that the Hindu or Buddhist notion of God is fundamentally different from ours. Moreover the attitude of people in these countries to eroticism and sexuality is also essentially different. Thus for example Indians primarily see nothing at all 'sinful' in either of these.

The 'Laws of Manu' occupy a special place in the Hindu smriti writings. They come from the post-Vedic period and regulate what we would call social and political questions. Human rights and duties are precisely defined in terms of castes, and women are given an absolutely subordinate status under men. (In the Vedic period there seems to have been an absolute equivalence of the sexes!)

The unconditional predominance of the Brahmans over all other people is one of the essential themes in the 'Laws of Manu'.

'Because the Brahman sprang from Brahma's mouth, because he is the firstborn and because he studies the Vedas, he is rightly regarded as lord of the whole world' (I.93).

So the 'Laws of Manu' are testimonies to the fixed social norms of Hinduism which still apply today. But above all the subordination of women to men and the unconditional pre-eminence of the Brahmans is laid down there.

An unbroken current of Hindu literature flows from the third millennium BCE to our era. It is a strange mixture of religion, philosophy and 'social teaching' in which now the religious and now the philosophical element predominates. So it would be artificial to want to divide this literature into religious, philosophical and socio-political writings; all these elements flow together in Hindu thought.

This also applies to the Darshanas, which have aptly been described as the branches of a tree, the trunk of which is formed by the four Vedas. The word Darshana comes from the Sanskrit and among other things means 'system'. What it denotes are the six schools of Hindu philosophy, which fundamentally all have one aim: liberation from rebirth and union with Brahman, the Absolute. Though the Darshanas, too, are in part hair-splitting philosophical speculations, in these texts there is continually clear evidence of the struggle for ethical principles focused on human society and its position in the universe as a whole.

The heroic epic is a special literary form in Hinduism; it is not really a religious work, but it conveys ideas which have their origin in the philosophical and religious sphere. We have already made the brief acquaintance of one of these epics in the Ramayana: Rama, Vishnu's avatar, fights against the demonic principle personified in King Ravana.

Another example of this genre is the Bhagavad Gita, of which it is rightly said that it is 'made of the stuff of Indian mysticism'. Today it is assumed that it was written down in the second century of our era, but parts of it may be essentially older.

Bhagavad Gita means 'song of the exalted one'. It is essentially a philosophical and religious didactic poem. The Western reader may at first be confused that the scene of the Bhagavad Gita is a battlefield on which, moreover, members of the same family confront one another. But it is the karma of the hero Arjuna which has driven him to battle.

Moreover the battlefield is the symbol of the constant battles which take place in human beings between the powers of good and evil, between their ego and their higher nature.

The framework of action of the Bhagavad Gita is as follows: Krishna – the avatar, the 'descent' of Vishnu – teaches Arjuna before the beginning of the great battle, which is really a family conflict, that all impressions which human beings take in from the world around them are transitory and in no way abiding. It is important to remain bold and steadfast in the face of them for the real, transcendent being.

> 'Anyone who believes that living beings kill or are killed is in ignorance. Anyone who is grounded in knowledge knows that living beings neither kill nor are killed.
>
> For the soul there is neither birth nor death. It also never ceases to be – as it once was. It is unborn, eternal, everlasting, immortal and primal. It is not killed when the body is struck' (Bhagavad Gita II, 19–20).

The 'soul' addressed in the Bhagavad Gita, an individual soul, is seen as a part of a spiritual whole. As Swami Prahupada has remarked, it tends 'to cover itself with illusory energy and so attain to corporeality'.

> 'One who is born is certain of death, and one who has died is certain of birth. Therefore you should not complain in the unavoidable fulfilment of your duty' (Bhagavad Gita II, 27).

> 'Just as fire is covered with smoke, so any concern is overshadowed by error. Therefore, son of Kunti, one should not give up the activity that springs from one's

own nature, even if such work is erroneous' (Bhagavad Gita XVIII, 48).

The fulfilment of the divine will – one of the main doctrines of the Bhagavad Gita – is one of the ways to the Absolute. This applies particularly to Arjuna, who is a member of the Kshatriya, the caste of warriors.

The Westerner may find the wealth of Hindu scriptures – and also their apparent contradictoriness – confusing. But Hindus seek – and find unity in – multiplicity. For Hindus, every notion is an aspect, even if our logic cannot make anything of it. The powerful religious and philosophical writings of Hinduism are a giant tree which has its roots in the Vedic scriptures and whose branches tower over the millennia to the present.

5

The Castes

The age-old social system of castes has been abolished in the constitution of the Republic of India, and officially no longer exists. But it continues unbroken in human hearts and even today governs the life of most Hindus.

First let us recall our own history, the rules of life which governed our own civilization. How many generations is it really since the nobility and the clergy were still strictly separated from 'the rest of the people'? What about the guilds and associations which on the one hand had to fulfil their duties strictly and on the other zealously defended their rights? Wasn't the social hierarchy a fixed structure in which there was little or no room for development? If we think in historical terms, all this is not so far back in the past. One could also ask whether elitist thought and action has in fact been completely overcome today.

But back to the Indian caste system. Its origin lies far in the past and had many causes. Here are two of the main ones.

When the peoples whom we describe under the summary term Indo-Aryans streamed over the hills into the Indus valley in the third millennium before our era, they were basically hordes of nomadic conquerors. Then they successively began to settle in more fertile areas. The conquerors, organized by tribes and clans without any central power, were very much in the minority compared with the conquered original population. So there was a fear that within a few generations they would be swallowed up. The first beginnings of the formation of castes can already be demonstrated at that time – still in the Vedic era. It is therefore certainly no coincidence that the Sanskrit word varna means 'caste' and at the same time 'colour'. We must therefore see the formation of castes as a measure to protect the purity of the race. However, this is only a partial explanation of this Hindu socio-political phenomenon.

The original society of the Indo-Aryan conquerors was by no means organized into states. The principles of order were the clan, the extended family and the tribe. Therefore the tribal leaders and the warriors were of decisive importance for the existence of communities; moreover they were the ones who maintained contact with the deities and had to assuage the angry powers of nature by sacrifices – and not a separate priesthood. Thus first of all a form of warrior nobility developed, which incidentally also had to perform religious tasks.

A further notion also gradually crystallized: every member of society was given clearly defined duties, corresponding to his capacities and situation. This led to a division of the population by the tasks and duties they had taken on. This was the second decisive reason for the origin of the Hindu caste system. We must not separate these two factors; beyond doubt they worked together and side by side.

At first the nobility and the warrior caste, the Kshatriyas, were at the uppermost level of the hierarchy; there was as yet no real priesthood. But in the course of time the conviction became established that the scrupulous, inerrant recitation of the sacrificial texts and the correct selection of them was of decisive influence for society, for either good or ill. The correct time, the correct selection of text, the correct emphasis on each individual syllable – all this was regarded as being vitally important. So 'specialists' developed who then controlled all the rites, which became more and more complicated, and handed down this knowledge only within their own family, i.e. to their sons. These 'specialists' then became the priesthood, and the caste of Brahmans came into being. Nor is it surprising that this 'elite' was anxiously concerned always and at all times to emphasize the vital importance of their knowledge and thus to increase their power. Thus in the end there was rivalry between the nobility and the priestly caste, which was becoming increasingly strong, over their status in the hierarchy. Many myths and legends bear eloquent testimony to the historical fact that this controversy was harsh and presumably often bloody. At the latest the 'Laws of Manu' show that the Brahmans emerged victoriously from these battles; at least for orthodoxy, they stand outside or above the law. It is expressly stated in the scriptures that a Brahman is holy and has a claim to veneration even if he commits shameful deeds.

A system of thought which seems almost manic, according to which everything in this life depends simply on the slavishly pedantic recitation of the ritual texts, brought the Brahmans their absolute pre-eminence in the social hierarchy. The old ritual texts are written in an archaic Sanskrit which hardly anyone understands any more.

Here involuntarily a comparison from our own culture presents itself: the Latin texts of the Christian ritual, too, were no longer understood by all priests and monks; quite often they were parroted, giving rise to so-called dog Latin, which often led to distortions of meaning.

This pre-eminence of the caste of Brahmans still exists in present-day modern India. However, the Brahmans today are by no means just priests; quite often they can be found in other professions, in business and in politics. But one is unlikely to find a Brahman in a socially subordinate position.

The caste which occupies second place in Hinduism is that of the Kshatriyas, the 'warriors'. The duty imposed on them by their karma is the defence of the law, the protection of the weak. These tasks suggest the ideals of Western chivalry. In the course of Indian history the Kshatriyas provided the kings and princes, the generals, the nobility and the aristocracy. As in European chivalry, honour, loyalty and the fulfilment of duty were the highest virtues of this caste. Their karma obligates them to activity, courage and unconditional performance of duty. This is clearly defined in the Bhagavad Gita. Thus Krishna says to Arjuna.

'Confronted with this task [the imminent battle, which is making Arjuna hesitate], you should know that there is no better activity for you than to fight on the basis of religious principles. Therefore you have truly no reason to hesitate' (Bhagavad Gita II, 31).

Krishna, the avatar of Vishnu, goes on to teach the Kshatriya Arjuna, who is still afraid before the battle against his clan and his friends:

'It is far better to do one's own prescribed duties than those of another. For even if one makes a mistake in the fulfilment of one's duties, or is even killed in the process, this is better than to do the duties of another, since it is dangerous to follow another's path' (Bhagavad Gita III, 35).

We can understand all these reflections only if we take in the notion of rebirth and the regularity of the web of karma.

Today members of the caste of Kshatriyas have turned to different professions. The Rajputs, who once also offered successful resistance to the advance of Islam, still live on in the old tradition as a 'warrior' caste. However, today the Rajput festivals have become a mere tourist attraction.

The third caste in the Hindu social order is that of the Vaishyas, who are essentially farmers and merchants. The duty imposed by their karma is to provide people with the necessary goods. Their obligation is the production and distribution of these basic materials. To use a term from our world, they form the 'middle class' within Indian society. Since in the course of history the Vaishyas learned largely to dominate trade, which increasingly flourished, it brought at least some of them considerable prosperity. On the other hand there is often deep need and wretchedness among the farmers who belong to this caste, though they are still better off than the country workers who are either Sudras, i.e. members of the next lower caste, or 'untouchables'.

The members of the castes of the Brahmans, the Kshatriyas and Vaishyas who have been discussed so far are called the 'twice-born', since their children – usually at the age of twelve – are solemnly accepted into their caste as full members and are thus born a second time.

The fourth caste, which is numerically by far the strongest, is that of the Sudras. Their karma obliges them to serve the members of the castes above them. They provide the auxiliary workers, servants, shepherds and also some of the craftsmen.

Contrary to widespread opinion the Sudras are not slaves; they are not owned and at least in theory can give up their activity at any time. They are also free in their choice of abode. But these remarks should not suggest a picture which is alien to reality. The 'freedoms' of the Sudras are usually of a very theoretical kind and can be put into practice only in the rarest cases.

The work of the Sudras can also be carried out by members of other castes. However, even a Sudra will not undertake particular activities – for example slaughtering, tanning and laying out the dead. These are left to the Pariahs, the 'untouchables'.

The duties assigned by karma, the inescapable causal law, to members of particular castes are clearly and unmistakably described and defined in the Bhagavad Gita, in Krishna's instructions to Arjuna:

'Brahmans, Kshatriyas, Vaishyas and Sudras differ by the characteristics of their action, which are related to the modes of appearance of their material nature . . .!'

'Peacefulness, self-control, continence, wisdom and piety are the characteristics which govern the actions of the Brahmans.'

'Courage, strength and resolution, skill, fearlessness in battle, generosity and the capacity to react are the characteristics which govern the actions of the Kshatriyas.'

'Agriculture, cattle-rearing and trade govern the actions of the Vaishyas, and the task of the Sudras is to perform physical labour and provide other services' (Bhagavad Gita XVIII, 41–45).

According to Hindu categories of thought, each person is reborn in accordance with the karma that he formed in his previous life. This karma determines whether he will be born into one of the castes or outside them. The four castes of the Brahmans, Kshatriyas, Vaishyas and Sudras form a well-defined social pyramid. A 'transfer' from one caste to another – so to speak a social improvement – is impossible within this life.

For the sake of completeness it should also be said that the four castes cited here represent only a framework. Within the individual castes, above all of the Vaishyas and the Sudras, there is a mass of 'sub-castes' which again are defined down to the smallest detail. Usually these are units defined by profession, like the caste of the goldsmiths. But even today all these divisions still have a decisive influence on the life of most Hindus.

The poorest of the poor are those without a caste, the Pariahs, the 'untouchables'. These are people whose karma determined that they would be born into no caste or who have lost their membership of a caste. The 'Laws of Manu' state:

> 'Illegitimate marriage between persons of different castes, marriages which are against the law, failure to perform the prescribed rites, all this is the origin of impurity.'

Loss of membership of a caste means expulsion from society, excommunication in the truest sense of the word. A Pariah was – and to some extent still is today – 'unclean' and despised. Mere contact with such a person makes others unclean, necessitating a complicated ritual of purification. Indeed in orthodoxy it is enough for the shadow of a Pariah to fall on the member of a caste to make him unclean. We can hardly imagine what all this must mean in a small village or market town. There the Pariahs were quite often avoided like wild animals, which still enjoyed great respect. Of course it is strictly forbidden for them to enter the temple; they would desecrate everything by their very presence. So basically they live outside society, outside the law and obligated only to the regulations for the 'untouchables'. These are regulations which we do better to call rules for survival. It is not putting it to harshly to say that Hindu orthodoxy sees Pariahs as beings between humans and animals – or even below the latter.

However, there were and are exceptions in the history of Hinduism to this contempt for the untouchables: some of the great 'saints' who are still worshipped today were Pariahs. Here it is evident that even systems which are maintained so strictly are broken through – though rarely. It should also be noted that the yogins, the sadhus, the sannyasins – the itinerant monks and 'holy men' – stand outside the caste system. The Sudras and the Pariahs are forbidden to study the sacred scriptures, but itinerant monks and ascetics are exempt from this prohibition. (However, where they belong to a lower caste, they will only rarely be able to read or write!)

One question which is hard to answer, if it can be answered at all, presents itself. Why does a member of a lower caste – or even a Pariah – not simply pretend to be something else? This seems to happen very rarely, evidently for two reasons. First, an impostor would be caught fairly quickly, because he would not have the appropriate education, could not have studied the Vedas and the other sacred scriptures, and his whole behaviour would soon betray him. Secondly, Hindus amazingly accept membership of a caste without resistance. This is probably because of the basic Hindu view which implies that the life lived in the present is the result of many previous lives and in turn is the basis for many more. For the Hindu it is a reality which is experienced deeply and taken for granted, a law from which he cannot think of breaking out. Moreover he sees no possibility of doing this.

In modern India the caste system has been abolished by the Indian constitution, but it has in no way disappeared from the hearts and minds of people. Nor in fact was that to be expected, since the social system in India built on the varna, the caste, is many centuries old and had been constantly in force. The great statesman and philosopher Mahatma Gandhi did a great deal for the Pariahs, the 'untouchables', and achieved some success. The term Harijan – 'angels of the deity' – for them comes from him. It was Gandhi who made sure that the Harijans could enter at least some of the great temples. This may seem an unimportant gesture to us Westerners, without significance for those concerned. But from the Indian perspective it must be rated a great success in terms of their social status in society. Thus some things have happened in twentieth-century India. However, not only there, a wide, almost unbridgeable gap yawns between the law and its practical implementation.

I have already mentioned the ramifications of the caste system in most sub-castes orientated on professions. They too demarcate themselves strictly from one another. So there is a colourful social mosaic that crosses this giant sub-continent like a close-meshed net – and also holds it captive. We Westerners should be aware that we can catch only a very incomplete glimpse of such a complicated social system, which has grown up over many centuries. So we must be careful with our judgments if we want to avoid prejudices.

In the course of Indian history there have been plenty of attempts to abolish or at least to weaken the caste system. Here we must content ourselves with discussing just a few of them, movements which still have had tangible effects.

Two attempts at reform were made as long as 2,500 years ago, prompted almost simultaneously by the excessive harshness of the Brahman social structure.

Buddha Shakyamuni, a prince and member of the caste of the Kshatriyas, saw himself first of all as a reformer within Hinduism, but then became founder of a new religion, a new philosophy, which rapidly conquered people's hearts. So Buddhism even became a state religion under the powerful Indian emperor Ashoka. (In noting such historical facts we should not forget that in India religion, philosophy and social policy have always been a unity.) The teaching of Buddha rejects the division of people by castes – and this has distinguished it from Hinduism from the start. This repudiation of a social system which had grown up might ultimately be the reason why after its initial blossoming Buddhism was again overgrown by Hinduism and almost totally vanished from India. It seems that the social order which had grown up since Vedic times re-established itself.

At about the same time as Buddha lived and taught – around 500 BCE – Mahavira proclaimed a doctrine from which the Jain religion was to develop. It too rejects the caste system. Jainism is still alive in India today. Granted, its followers are not very numerous, but most of them are prosperous and influential.

Alongside these two movements which undertook a socio-political revolution – or attempted one – we should note a phenomenon which has substantially influenced Indian history over the last few centuries: the unbridgeable hostility between Hindus and Muslims is certainly to be derived from the rejection of the 'abhorrent' polytheism of the Hindus by Islam. But in this context it is easy to forget that there is another side to this token of repudiation: Islam has no caste system and rejects it unconditionally. From a Hindu perspective it must therefore be regarded as 'destructive of society' and fought against. The irreconcilable enmity between Islam and Hinduism thus has socio-political motives as well as religious and theological ones. Here there has been no lack of attempts to arrive at a compromise solution between the two hostile camps. One especially significant figure in this context was the Mogul emperor Akbar – who was a Muslim. However, his attempt, motivated by great tolerance, ended without success and had no lasting effect.

The reform movement of Guru Nanak, the founder of the Sikh movement, fared rather differently. The Sikhs have taken over monotheistic thought from Islam and rejected the caste system. Interestingly, originally the Sikh community was pacifist and rejected any use of violence. Evidently as a result of lasting hostility and persecution, this attitude turned into its opposite. The Sikhs are uncompromising fighters and are known and feared as such. In particular in the present it is evident that some Sikhs tend towards extremism and even terrorism. This fanatical trait in the Sikh movement has only intensified since the partial destruction of their sanctuary in Amritsar by the Indian government. It cost Indira Gandhi her life.

In the course of the long history of Hinduism, there have been no lack of attempts to break through the rigid social system of the Hindu castes. Of the many such movements, mention has been made here of Buddhism, Jainism, the thought world of the Mogul emperor Akbar and the religion of the Sikhs. I have attempted to show that here ideas about changing the social system have played a role alongside philosophical and theological perspectives.

In addition it should also be said that in the orthodox view one cannot become a Hindu. To be one one must have been born into a caste by rebirth.

The determining element in the Hindu social order, the caste system, is age-old; its beginnings can be traced back to Vedic times. It came into being on the one hand as a 'measure to protect the purity of the race' and on the other out of a need to show everyone their duties and rights. Whereas at first the aristocratic caste of the Kshatriyas stood at the summit of the social pyramid, the rising priesthood could present itself as those who were most important for the survival of society. They finally proved victorious in the battle for pre-eminence; the Brahman caste elevated itself above all the others, and set itself above the law. The two other castes, the Vaishas and the Sudras, sub-divided into many sub-castes which are determined by profession. This complicated net has an extremely narrow mesh, so that for example marriages between members of different castes are tabu. The poorest of the poor are the 'untouchables', the Pariahs, whom Mahatma Gandhi called the Harijans, the 'angels of the deity'.

6

Death and Rebirth

The Hindu notions of death and rebirth are the expression of a 'cyclical' view of the world. In the cycle of earthly manifestations there is no beginning and therefore no end.

When human evolution had reached a stage when it became possible for people to reflect about themselves, it began: human beings could not come to terms with their evident finitude. The ideas that they produced to find a way out of their dilemma run into thousands and show how longingly – and also how doggedly – the brains of many generations have sought a solution. The problem of the finitude of human existence was probably one of the motivations for the origin of religions – though not the only one. This is not the place to discuss the countless number of cults of the dead – they are an expression of ideas of a beyond, a life after death. Here I shall limit myself to the thought-world of Hinduism, in which the idea of rebirth has a leading significance.

What, according to Hindu ideas, is really reborn? The way we Westerners think is shaped by our notion of the Christian duality of body and soul. Whereas the former, as the 'vessel of the soul', is transitory, the soul remains timeless and thus eternal. Here we begin from an individual soul; in other words, to put it simply, the self, this quite personal individual 'I', lives on after our death to all eternity.

The Hindu thinks differently: the atman, this 'particle' of the absolute Brahman which is to be found in any being – at least in orthodox philosophical thought – has no individuality; after death, the atman indwelling human beings returns to the Brahman, the absolute, and fuses with it.

The tat tvam asi, the 'That is what you are' of the Upanishads, means that the atman, the 'breath of the Absolute' in human beings, is what is real and essential. Purusha and prakriti make it jiva, the relative and therefore suffering individual, but atman makes this individual participate in absoluteness, non-duality. However – and this is the decisive thing – atman in human beings is not the 'individual soul' that Christian thought knows.

This excursion into orthodox Hindu philosophy, which is alien to us, was necessary to get nearer to the question 'What, according to Hindu ideas, is really reborn?'

Let us remind ourselves of what was said about the concept of karma, the principle of causality in Indian thought. The web of karma – formed in the present life and the many lives that preceded it – is the immediate cause of rebirth, and it too is what is reborn. To translate this into our categories of thought, we can imagine that actions or failures to act in life, i.e. in the sphere of the non-absolute, produce fields of tension which seek resolution, which are 'charged with energy'. This difference of potential and the energy resulting from it is what is reborn.

Another comparison we might understand – though like all comparisons it is problematical and incomplete – would be this: in the sphere of the non-Absolute, i.e. in life, dissonances arises which seek harmonic resolution. These 'dissonances in life' and the energy peculiar to them extend from one life into the next and are also its cause. Only the dissolution of the web of karma in identification with dharma, the absolute law of the universe, will break through the cycle of rebirths and become Brahman-nirvana.

As I have already indicated, this is not a place, a 'heaven'; it is a state in the sphere of the Absolute and therefore one which cannot be described, since it has no characteristics in the sense of polarity. According to the teachings of Hindu philosophy – above all the Upanishads – this makes the question of the character of nirvana superfluous; as there is no duality, the question of being or non-being is also irrelevant and cannot be put.

Here again we are in the realm of philosophy, and it should be pointed out that while these notions are there, 'underground' in popular belief – whatever we are to understand by that –, they have a more simplified and distorted, 'adapted' form.

Hindus see themselves as part of a multiplicity which for them is a unity. So they see their lives as one of many, and their deaths as the gateway to the next life.

At all events, the idea of rebirth leads to death not being 'repressed' in Hinduism, as has come to be the fashion in our cultural circles.

Funeral customs in Hinduism are essentially governed by an age-old symbolism of the elements and thus reflect the notion of being embedded in nature. The corpse is burnt, and when possible the ashes are sprinkled on the surface of a 'sacred' stretch of water. Thus the element of fire purifies the mortal element and conveys it to the 'world ether', while the ash returns in the element of water to the eternal cycle of the universe. Sometimes the ashes are put in the earth. Here too the symbolism of the elements is decisive.

Believing Hindus know places which are regarded as especially meritorious for one's karma. One particularly well-known such place is the city of Varanasi, which we call Benares. Thus even today many old people who feel that their end is near often travel great distances to this place in order to spend the last time allotted to them here and then to die and be turned to ashes. Varanasi has been a 'sacred' place of great spiritual and cultic significance since human thought began. It is on the 'sacred river' Ganges, 'mother Ganga'. As the river there flows almost precisely in a south-north direction, in the morning the many believers who direct their devotions to the ghats on the left bank of the Ganges are looking towards the sun rising in the East. When they see the sun rising over the horizon, in deep devotion they offer their prayers and perform purification rituals in the 'sacred' river. On the left bank are also the two ghats for cremations; there the flames of the fire flicker which restores people to the universe, going beyond the transitory in the cycle of all being.

The ghats of Varanasi – and the burning places – have now become a kind of tourist attraction. The travel agencies carry tourists in buses there early in the morning, and boats are hired which go alongside the terraces to give the foreigners good opportunities for photographs. However, this evidently does not disturb the many pious pilgrims very much. In Hindu thought, as we have seen, secular and sacred lie very close together, and no real distinction is made here. That is also evident in the fact that giant advertisements for electrical equipment or soft drinks adorn the walls of the palaces along the ghats, in no way falling short of the depictions of Shiva in their colourfulness.

One particular feature should be mentioned here in passing, since it is very characteristic of Hinduism: the palaces of the maharajahs and the rich, built as accommodation for their pilgrimages here, rise closely packed along the left bank of the Ganges. However, one of the greatest and most luxurious palaces belongs to a man who sells the 'sacred fire' for burning corpses. He belongs to a lowly caste, but is nevertheless one of the richest men in Varanasi. His office has come down to him as a hereditary one over many generations. We see only the male relatives of the dead person at the pyres of the ghats where bodies are burned; it is the sacred duty of the oldest son to kindle the flame. For this he needs the 'sacred fire', which he buys in a special temple. The seller has no fixed prices, but estimates the purchasing power of his customers and asks what he thinks possible. This is by no means always cash, but sometimes can also be farmland. No wonder that this seller of 'sacred fire' is allegedly also one of the greatest landowners! It is hard for us to understand how this business can still go on as it has done for centuries.

At the cremation ghats of Varanasi it is easy for the perceptive observer to notice that in Hinduism too, death does not make all people 'equal'. Rich relatives buy expensive, sweet-smelling sandal wood for cremating their kin, while the poor even during their lifetime laboriously gather any gnarled branches and guard this stock of wood like a precious treasure. In the numerous shops in the alleyways above the ghats one can get carefully measured quanties of sandalwood chips to throw into the flames. They are sold in plastic bags, so the new age has dawned! There are also a variety of heavy sacks, since of course account must be taken of everyone's purchasing power.

Now the idea of an equality in death is also a typically Western one. If we remember the doctrine of karma, the different webs of karma and the rebirth that results from this, any notion of equality is nonsensical. This idea of differences governed by karma also explains why Communism found comparatively little support in Hindu countries.

There are severe penalties in present-day India for suttee, the burning of widows, made known in the West particularly through Jules Verne's *Around the World in Eighty Days*, but it is said still to be practised in remote areas. The fact that a woman – voluntarily – would allow herself to be burnt alive on a pyre with the corpse of her husband seems quite unimaginable, incomprehensible and barbaric to us. However, the question remains whether we have the right to condemn the custom. Certainly according to the orthodox Hindu view, if a widow is not the mother of sons she has no rights. She is taken neither into the family of her dead husband nor into her own and usually leads a wretched life. She must be glad to be able to have a more than modest existence as a serving woman. But if she mounts her husband's pyre, then his family builds her a sacrificial altar, and perhaps even a temple. Then every day flowers and grains of corn are offered to her as a sacrifice – as to a saint. With her voluntary death she has fulfilled her karma, and can be certain of a better rebirth.

> **Atman, which is infinitely fine, is the real essence in human beings, the true reality; that is what you yourself are, tat tvam asi. But death is an ingredient of life.**

7

Monks, Saints and Ascetics

A 'clerical hierarchy' is alien to Hinduism, though the priestly caste of the Brahmans is still unchallenged today. The monasticism which is marked in India does not have a central organization either, nor does it have a hierarchical structure in the sense of a hierarchy expressed in titles. So the various designations, which are not in fact 'bestowed', run into one another. This chapter attempts to explain the different 'kinds' of Hindu monk. However, a clear binding definition will prove impossible.

The sannyasin is a man who has renounced the world and without a fixed abode or personal possessions lives with just one aim: he wants to attain moksha, enlightenment, or at least come close to it. We should recall that moksha is liberation from any worldly ties, from all feelings which go with it like love, hatred, interest or antipathy, willing and desiring, and so on. For the one who has attained moksha the cycle of rebirths is extinguished, and the state of nirvana, being in absoluteness, is open.

Nowadays the term sannyasin has been considerably devalued, since it is also applied to any itinerant beggar, however uneducated and primitive. The cause of this is its application by Western followers to their modern gurus. An apt comparison has been made: 'If a mouse is called an elephant, then the word "elephant" loses its value as a clear designation of an actual elephant and thus language loses its function as a means of communication.' We can certainly extend the point further and apply it to terms like guru, bhagavan, yogi, baba and swami.

However, back to the sannyasin. He usually wears a white or yellow monastic garment and shows his ishta devata, his personal ideal of God, by the painting on his forehead. Horizontal stripes – usually a red one between two white ones – show him to be a Shivaite, and vertical ones to be a Vishnuite. He travels through the country and also sometimes spends time in an ashram, a pilgrim lodging, on his way, gaining his scanty sustenance by begging. Sometimes he can also be found in a lonely place or a cave, devoted to meditation.

How does someone become a sannyasin? There is no prescribed rule, no defined process here. It may happen that a young man – still almost a boy – decides to 'renounce the world'. His family holds something like a funeral for him and then he leaves the family bonds; his relatives will never see him again. The youngster then travels round the land – his garment and his begging bowl are his only possessions. He will seek a guru, a spiritual teacher, to help him on his quest for truth. He will live without a fixed abode and without possessions and – if his karma is prepared accordingly – one day he will attain moksha.

Some of the Hindu itinerant monks have a different past. They follow – even today – an age-old custom which, quite simply, is this. There are three periods in a man's life. In the first, as a child and young person he has to learn to lead his own life. In the second he will have a family and bring children – above all sons – into the world. But once these have become independent the family no longer needs the father to support it and the third period begins. One day he will leave his hut and his family silently and unnoticed and wander off without possessions. As a begging monk he will see his task now as only to prepare for death and thus for his next life, to purify his karma and approach his ishta devata.

The yogins – they see Shiva in his aspect of Mahayogin as their model, their ishta devata – have chosen the most varied forms of asceticism as a way to enlightenment. The word yoga is derived from a Sanskrit term which means 'yoke'. There are different schools of yoga, and a whole series of grades with in them. Yoga exercises are not just physical exercises, as is usually assumed in the West. For the Hindu these – which are called Hatha Yoga – are merely preludes to other exercises. Yoga involves spirit and body equally and ultimately has purely spiritual aims.

One can find the ascetic, usually naked figures of the Shivaite yogins all over India. The sit in the lotus position, with legs crossed under them, apparently oblivious to their surroundings, whether in some great Indian city or high up on the edge of the glaciers of the Himalayas. There are serious reports that these people can produce 'inner warmth' in deep yoga meditation which makes it possible for them to survive in extreme mountain regions. Here, too, we find capacities which we Westerners are fond of calling 'supernatural'. But the Hindu sees them as quite natural.

Here something needs to be said about the term 'fakir'. This word derives from Arabic and means 'the poor one'. It is unknown in Hindu terminology; we Westerners have taken this term, which derives from the mystical world of the Islamic dervishes, to India almost as an artefact.

The 'penitents' who on different Hindu festivals pierce their bodies with needles, flog themselves and torment themselves in every conceivable way. strike a particular echo in Western observers. In essence these spectacular actions have nothing to do with Hinduism; they are excesses tolerated by the majority of Hindus, but usually repudiated and not understood. Western observers would do well not to draw direct conclusions from such 'sensational' pictures to Hindu categories of thought.

A further designation of Hindu itinerant monks is sadhu. The Sanskrit word sadh is best rendered 'lead to a goal'. The sadhu is also a God-seeker, someone in quest of fulfilment, who has renounced the world. The term sadhu is also hard to define or to distinguish from other terms.

The sadhus include men of very different origin and levels of education. Quite often they are very simple people, often unable to read or write, so they cannot study the scriptures either. They stand outside the caste system and it is regarded as meritorious to give them alms.

Here it should be noted that in the Hindu view it is not the one who receives alms but the giver who has to be grateful: he has been offered an opportunity to improve his karma by his compassion.

Another term which has by now also become known in the West is swami. This word really denotes a 'master', comparable to the English 'Sir'. If the word swami is put before a name, then it is also meant in this sense. Put after the name it is an honorific title used above all in addressing 'holy' and learned men. It is not bestowed by any institution, nor is it associated with particular examinations. Someone will one day use this form of address to the person concerned, and the more revered and acknowledged the holy man is, the more quickly it will become established.

Westerners will wonder about the possible misuse of such honorific titles. It is probably almost impossible to give any kind of correct estimate of the frequency of charlatans. But we shall hardly go wrong in assuming that there are also some very shady figures among the 'holy men' active in the West. However, for Hindus the question seems either not to exist or to be insignificant.

The address 'Baba' is used towards revered men and corresponds to our 'father'. The address 'Bhagavan' is used equally respectfully by disciples to their especially revered guru. Bhagavan really means 'exalted one', 'holy', and is also used as a form of address to a deity.

In the West the term guru has become common usage, so as a result it has suffered some distortion and devaluation. One should not call a mouse an elephant! That makes the word elephant senseless and misleading. The same is probably the case with guru. So I shall go more closely into the term guru and the Hindu tradition which underlies it.

Four levels of 'guru' are distinguished:

1. The parents who provide us with our bodies and introduce us to the problems of life;
2. Worldly teachers, master craftsmen and educators;
3. The spiritual teacher who explains the meaning of being to us and points the way towards realization of the self;
4. The cosmic guru, the ishta devata, to which our spiritual master leads us.

The guru in the narrower sense of the word is thus a spiritual teacher, though no spiritual piggy-back is possible: the guru can show a person the way, but that person must travel it alone.

Time and again it is asked whether the disciple really owes unconditional obedience to his guru. The scriptures say that it would be completely senseless to obey a guru against one's own will. Only if obedience is the expression and emanation of authentic trust will the disciple-teacher relationship also lead to the desired goal. It is evident that such a relationship can also be misused.

Alongside the monks and holy men discussed here, who have had no kind of priestly consecration and do not exercise any cultic functions, there is also a professional priesthood, the Brahmans, who perform cultic services at one of the many temples. They celebrate the rituals, and have their functions in initiating a young person into his caste, at weddings, cremations and religious festivals. They also give advice to believers – of course for an appropriate fee – about all matters of life. Thus for example one can see them sitting under parasols at the ghats in Varanasi. The usually penniless pilgrims surround them to get advice and blessing.

Even today the Brahmans still enjoy great respect and reverence. It would not occur, for example, to a non-Brahman to perform his ritual washing at a place reserved for the caste of Brahmans. So larger temples have two 'sacred pools', one for the Brahmans and one for the rest of the people. However, again the 'untouchables', the Pariahs, are excluded from these. Nor are any ritual washings and baths prescribed for them.

What about the women? By and large Hindu 'holiness' – in accordance with the 'Laws of Manu' – is still a masculine domain. However, one does also find isolated instances of women who follow the call to holiness and live the life of nuns. Otherwise it is the religious task of the woman to decorate the domestic altar which can be found in every hut with flowers and also set out grains of rice or corn as an offering. One can also see women taking part in ritual actions in the temples or at the ghats by the sacred rivers. One can witness a special scene in the temple of Durga when young mothers show their children to the god as the result of their prayers to him. The breasts of Durga are first anointed with butter and then sprinkled with water. All in all the religious role of the woman in Hinduism is more a passive one; the great rituals are still purely the domain of men.

Just as the world of the Hindu gods is a manifold one, so the palette of holy men is also colourful. All these sannyasins, yogins, swamis, babas and bhagavans are very difficult to tell apart, as they are not institutionalized in our terms. The term guru is to be understood as a 'spiritual guide' in the narrower sense. The Brahmans are the professional priests. They perform the many different rituals which are required in the life of a Hindu. They are regarded as 'holy men' by virtue of their birth and enjoy great respect and high esteem even in present-day India. Women take part in ritual actions, but they are assigned a more passive role. Their main religious duty is to take care of the domestic altar.

8

The Hindu Temple – A Mystical, Three-Dimensional Diagram

The building plan underlying the Hindu temple is an expression of an age-old mystical basic concept: the square – sometimes also the right angle – symbolizes the abstract worlds; it is felt to be a clear, immovable, final form and is fixed by 'cardinal points'. The square is thus a mystical symbol for Brahman, for absoluteness. The circle is different: it stands for the earthly, for movement and the cycle of the ages. The equilateral triangle standing on its base symbolizes the male and standing on its apex symbolizes the female. The two triangles superimposed on each other – the 'star of David' – are an expression of the overcoming of polarity and thus again of the absoluteness of Brahman.

This canon of forms – together with a mystical symbolism of the points of the compass – is basically to be found in any Hindu temple, whether this is just a small village temple or one of the great well-known temple complexes.

It should be noted here that great similarities or at least analogies are to be found to the basic mystical forms of sacred buildings in a wide variety of religions and cultures.

One fundamental principle is characteristic of almost all Hindu temples: the basic division into a small room with a statue or the symbol of the divine being worshipped and the more or less large room in which believers gather. These two spatial units are connected by a corridor which is usually low and narrow. It is significant that the 'cella', the main sanctuary with its representation of the deity, is small and offers no place for believers. Only a few select priests – Brahmans – will enter this holy of holies and celebrate the real, 'intimate' sacrifice. The people are not admitted to this innermost sanctuary; they have to stay in the hall of assembly before the garbha griha – as the 'cella' is called (literally 'womb-house') – during the cult. The basic division outlined here can be found in all Hindu temples, with very few exceptions. In large complexes there are yet other buildings, as for example the 'house of the dancing maidens'. Communication centres are also provided, since pilgrims often travel great distances to temples and spend a certain amount of time there. As with us, market stalls are grouped round the temple proper with all kinds of goods for sale, including one or more Yajur Veda pharmacists. All kinds of medicines which have an age-old tradition are sold there. They are made from plants, but also from animals, for example snake venom or powdered lizard bones. The whole atmosphere is noisy and colourful. Here, too, the profoundly religious and the secular lie side by side.

However, to return to the temple proper: the garbha griha, the innermost sanctuary, has a tower built on it which is called the sikhara. These towers – which can be found in most cultures – represent the world mountain Meru. They are to be seen as' axes' which link the three levels of the world: the superterrestrial, the terrestrial and the subterranean.

First let us visit the garbha griha, for example of a Shiva temple, once again. In front of the building proper we shall be struck by Nandi, the white bull, the symbolic mount of Shiva. Inside, we shall again encounter the depiction of the

lingam yoni, the symbolic representation of the overcoming
of polarity. Lingam and yoni are smeared with blood;
water, constantly poured over the symbolic statuary, is
given to the pilgrims – or even sold. They will take this water
home and be convinced of its miraculous power. Our visit
inside the temple will be accompanied by the persistent
ringing of a bell: every believer who enters the temple strikes
the bell. On the one hand it announces his arrival to the
deity, but on the other hand it shows him that he is now
entering a different, spiritual, mystical world. In the temple
the pilgrims say their prayers, sing hymns and constantly
repeat the sacred Hari Om. I have already mentioned the
term Hari. Om is the mantra which is used most frequently.
This word is difficult to explain, and is a so-called 'root
syllable', a primal sound to which mystical power is
attributed. A mantra is also an 'inward summary' of the
properties of the ishta devata. In the Hindu view the
constant repetition of a mantra purifies thought and opens
up the possibility of concentrating on a deity.

As a foreigner and a non-Hindu one is not always allowed
to enter a Hindu temple, but this can happen now and then.
In one of the shops in front of the temple one may have
found a tablet with the traditional sacrificial gifts – flowers
and grains of corn – and will then have brought this into the
sanctuary in honour of some divine quest. If one has
behaved appropriately, the Brahman will also press a red
spot on one's forehead. Contrary to a view widespread in
the West, this red spot has nothing at all to do with the
status of the family. It is placed on the forehead of both
women and men in sacrificial rituals or – only in the case of
women – simply worn as an ornament. Family status is
often indicated quite differently – married women dye the
crowns of their heads with red henna.

But to return to the Hindu temple. Before entering a
sanctuary we must not fail to take off anything made of

leather or which looks like leather. Not to do so would be regarded by the local people as a great insult to the deity.

In the West the 'decorations' on some Indian temples enjoy a considerable degree of notoriety. The often very skilful erotic sculptures have been – and often still are – regarded as 'obscene', 'primitive' and 'pagan' and dismissed. However, the question arises to what extent such sculptures, often carried out to perfection, need any 'justification' from us, as though they were blasphemy or worse. In the brief discussion of Tantric thought in Shaktism I have already pointed out that sexuality and its depiction is a symbol of the duality and polarity of the relative sphere in which the life that human beings can perceive is encapsulated. For the Tantrics the sexual act – the yab-yum representation – symbolizes this relativity in the absoluteness of Brahman. Moreover from time immemorial, Hindus have had an attitude to eroticism and sexuality fundamentally different from ours, which cannot primarily be seen as sin. However, this 'free' attitude is not without a certain ambivalence; in the Hindu sphere, too, there are trends in which bodily asceticism is required, glorified and revered.

Ritual actions are by no means bound to the temple. They can also be carried out in the open air, especially on the banks of sacred rivers. It is gripping for us Westerners, too, when believers gather on the banks of a river, sing their hymns, wave torches and set afloat little boats made of lotus leaves containing flowers and a lighted candle.

The Hindu temple is a building erected according to given rules of mystical architecture. The essential feature, which is recognizable in any temple, is the distinction between a 'holy of holies', the garba griha with the symbol of the deity, and a room in which the faithful gather. The tower above the garbha griha, the sikhara, is to be understood as a symbol of the 'world mountain', the mountain Meru. Worship consists in the singing of hymns and sacrificial ceremonies. The latter derive from an age-old symbolism of the elements which goes back to Vedic times. Erotic representations on the temple walls are an expression of Tantric thought and a completely different attitude to eroticism and sexuality from ours. Ritual actions in Hinduism are by no means limited to the temple. Indian piety also finds compelling expression in the open air.

9

Hinduism – A Complex Form of Life

If we want to understand life within the Indian sub-continent, which is dominated by Hinduism, we must begin from two basic presuppositions. First, there is no 'uniform' Hinduism; for millennia these people have sought unity in multiplicity. Thus a system has developed which we find remarkably undogmatic but which offers each individual his personal way and leaves it open.

However, this shimmering multiplicity that we often find confusing flourishes on a clear, not to say rigid, matrix, which can be summed up in the following points:

All phenomena which are accessible to the human senses belong to a relative sphere; in other words, they are dependent and therefore untrue in the sense of the Absolute. So the Hindu calls them maya, illusion.

The absolute, Brahman, is on the one hand not accessible to human beings, but on the other is present in each person as a particle, as atman.

The earthly, and therefore relative, sphere in which we live is subject to the law of causality (karma). This unconditional causality is the driving force behind all being; it is cause and effect at the same time.

The notion of karma leads to the absolute assumption of rebirth.

It is the destiny of human beings, their karma, to approach dharma, the absolute law of the universe. The goal must be to demolish karma, or allow oneself to become identical with dharma. Then Brahman-nirvana is attained, the polarity characteristic of the relative sphere is overcome and thus loses its object; the cycle of rebirth is broken through.

At first these reflections sound complicated and 'academic'. But Hindus take them for granted; they are as it were part of the world of their experience. However, there are quite major differences between the thought-worlds of deeply spiritual and educated men and that of the simple 'man in the street'. But these five points are without qualification part of the self-understanding of the latter.

Even the simplest person somewhere on the broad Indian sub-continent 'knows' that Brahman, which is also to be found in him as atman, cannot be 'comprehensible' to him. So he needs the aspects, the 'reflections' of absoluteness: the gods. It is now open to him to chose as ishta devata that being which seems to him to be most helpful on his spiritual way. So he becomes a Vishnuite or a Shivaite. For him his ishta devata is the supreme guru in his life.

It is also important for us to remember that in Hinduism there is no sharp dividing line between religion and secular life. Religion, philosophy, life-style to the point of the those areas which we would call politics in the narrower or broader sense, form an indissoluble unity for the Indians, which determine their being.

Here two factors need to be noted which are not a matter of course for us. Asians in general and Indians in particular have a characteristic trait which is usually described as 'piety'. This is a marked sense for spirituality, a property which people in the industrialized countries have largely lost. The foundation of this spirituality is the knowledge of being embedded in the totality of the universe.

Hindus live in a world stamped by age-old traditions. They are still products of their culture and tradition, which is thousands of years old, and have never lost the sense of this, even if some may no longer know its origins. As one of the many possible examples, mention might be made here of a phenomenon with which anyone travelling to India is confronted: the so-called 'sacred cow'. The Sanskrit word go has several meanings: it means 'cow', but also 'forehead', 'ray' and 'earth'. How the 'sacred cow' of India has developed into a tradition cannot be clearly explained from these etymologies, and there are also very different views on the question. (Goloka, 'the place of the cow', is seen as the seat of Vishnu!) The most common view sees the 'sacred cow' as a symbol for the 'giver of life'. The example chosen here is meant to indicate how Indians are rooted in age-old traditions, which it is no longer possible to define clearly.

Complex though Hinduism may be as an ideology, the struggle for basic ethical and moral values is clear time and again. But in this respect, too, it will seem to us that there are contradictions and illogicalities. For example there is the idea of bhakti, the loving devotion shown not only to the deity but also to all living creatures on the one hand, and the instructions of Krishna, the avatar of Vishnu, to Arjuna before the battle in the Bhagavad Gita on the other. We must also see a contradiction in the absolute prohibition against killing which in some Hindu schools leads to a consistent vegetarianism, and the use of animal sacrifices which must be offered to some gods or goddess. Here – as also in other cases – we can note that our Western logic is not applicable. (We should not, however, apply any value judgments here.)

Time and again attention is drawn to the particularly tolerant attitude of Hindus to those of other faiths. This is correct – at least partially. We Westerners are in search of the one truth, whereas Hindus know that many truths form a unity.

It cannot be the task of this book to discuss the social situation in the Republic of India at any length, but here an example can be given of the consequences of the excessively strong bond with tradition in Hinduism.

Especially in the flat lands, it is regarded as a misfortune for a daughter to be born. The main reason for this is simply that the marriage of a daughter often amounts to a financial catastrophe. The expense of such a ceremony which is traditionally required often leads to financial ruin for the whole family. The farmer must take out a loan from richer landowners and pledge his own land. The very high rate of interest required often makes repayment impossible, and the pledged land falls to the creditor, who thus becomes even richer, while the father of the bride then sometimes has to work as a day labourer on his former property. Such 'land speculations' are often also a reason for leaving the land. The former farmer who has lost his land seeks his fortune in the city and then with a probability bordering on certainty contributes to the growth of the slums. Furthermore – especially in Calcutta – there is also the refugee problem: thousands of people from Bangladesh flee from the cruel distress in their country and seek their salvation – almost always in vain – in the giant city.

Hindu thought rooted in tradition has a negative effect today in yet another respect. For many centuries the extended family has functioned within the predominantly farming society and thus also provided a kind of welfare system in old age. It was simply important to have many children – sons! – in order to be looked after in old age. This notion, deeply rooted in people, still has a marked effect today, but the system no longer functions. It has turned into its opposite: with the present-day density of population the ground that can be cultivated – still without technical and chemical means – is simply no longer enough to feed people, and the increase in population causes hunger. However, the old system, 'having as many children as possible', which no longer functions, is still there unbroken in people's minds, conditioned by tradition. So any attempt at birth control is doomed to failure.

It would of course be very superficial and cheap to make 'religion' responsible for the wretchedness and misery of India and therefore to want to abolish it. Quite apart from the fact that it is utterly naive to imagine such a demand being carried out, the question arises how the resultant vacuum could then be filled. It is a simple fact that present-day Indians are the products of a culture in the broadest sense of the word which is thousands of year old. They are imprisoned in it and rooted in it; it is the basis of their being, regardless of the degree of their education, their material standard or their profession. The roots of their being lie in the sanatana dharma, the 'eternal' law, which in whatever form represents the basis of their existence.

So the rapid increase in the population of the Indian subcontinent confronts people with the infinitely difficult task of bringing their culture, their view of life, their world-view, into line with the ideology of the age of technology. They will not succeed without help from outside, but at the same time a danger can be seen here. Will the West – or rather, the industrialized countries – in fact succeed in acting subtly here and not simply put material advantage above all else, as in the days of colonization? If we are to have any degree of optimism about this development in the interest of humankind, then one thing is absolutely neces-sary: the abolition of all prejudices against alien ways of thinking, which beyond question still cling to us from the days of colonial rule.

Hindu thought does not distinguish between religious and secular phenomena, but constantly seeks unity in confusing plurality. There is no separation between religion and politics in the wider or the narrower sense. Even today, age-old traditions still determine people's lives, though from a present-day perspective they must seem to be to their disadvantage. Within a colourful, shimmering plurality the thought model underlying the sanatana dharma is orientated on the 'all-one' of Brahman, the Absolute.

Glossary

Amrita	Literally 'immortal'; water of life, sometimes identified with soma.
Arjuna	Literally 'white': hero of the Bhagavad Gita; Krishna, the avatar of Vishnu, speaks to him.
Ashram	Lodging, also a centre for spiritual exercises.
Atman	The 'real self' in the human being, a particle of Brahman; with qualifications, comparable to the Christian notion of the soul.
Avatar	Literally 'descent': incarnation of divine consciousness on earth. Vishnu is incarnate in ten avatars, the last of which – Kalki – will appear at the end of our world-age.
Bhagavad Gita	Literally, 'song of the exalted', a philosophical didactic poem composed between the fifth century BCE and the second century CE. Krishna, the avatar of Vishnu, instructs the hero Arjuna.
Bhairava	The 'terrifying' aspect of Shiva.
Bhairavi	The 'terrifying' aspect of Parvati, the consort of Shiva.

Bhakti	Devotion to the deity, but also to all fellow-creatures; an essential ideal in Vishnuism.
Brahma	A deity in the Hindu trimurti, God in his aspect as creator of the universe, represented with four heads and four arms.
Brahman	The non-dual reality without properties, resting in itself, the Absolute; as a pure abstraction inaccessible to human thought. Brahman is subject, not object.
Brahmans	Members of the priestly caste, occupying first place in the caste system.
Darshana	Literally 'gaze', 'see', also 'system'; six schools of Hindu philosophy.
Dharma	Literally 'bear', 'hold'. The law of the universe, the foundation of any human ethic and morality. Hindus call their religion sanatana dharma, the 'eternal law'.
Durga	Literally 'unfathomable'. An age-old designation for the divine mother; shakti of Shiva, usually represented with ten arms; destroys the demon of not-knowing. Often fused into one being with Kali.
Ganesha	Also Ganapati, god of wisdom depicted with an elephant head; also the 'remover of obstacles' and 'preparer of ways', son of Parvati and Shiva.

Ganga	Female personification of the Ganges, 'Mother Ganga'.
Garba griha	Innermost sanctuary in the Hindu temple.
Ghat	Terraced site leading down to a river or lake; access to the element of water, place of rituals of purification but also for washing; some ghats are reserved for cremating corpses, after which the ashes are committed to the element of water.
Go	Sanskrit word meaning 1. cow; 2. forehead, ray, light; 3.earth. Designation for the 'sacred cow'.
Guru	Spiritual teacher and master. It is his task to show the way to his disciple but not to disseminate a doctrine.
Guru Nanak	Founder of the Sikh movement (1469 to 1538).
Hanuman	Also Hanumat. Deity in the form of a monkey. 'The one with the strong jowl'; Rama's helper in the battle against Ravana in the Ramayana epic; probably derived from a military standard; enjoys great popularity in present-day Hinduism.
Hara	Another name for Shiva.
Hari	Another name for Vishnu.
Harijan	'Angel of the deity'; designation of Mahatma Gandhi for the Pariahs, the 'untouchables'.

Ishta devata	Literally Ishta, 'beloved', 'wish'; deva, 'god'. Is often translated 'chosen ideal': personally chosen aspect of Brahman, the Absolute, the aspect that is to be worshipped.
Ishvara	'Lord of the universe; literally ish, 'rule'. Notion of the personal God as creator, since human beings can only grasp deities with a form.
Jain, Jainism	Pre-Christian religion founded by Mahavira in the fifth century BCE, rejects the authority of the Vedas.
Jati	Hindu term for caste.
Jiva	From the Sansrit jiv, 'live'; some-one living in a body; the embodied self which is bound to the cycle of rebirths.
Kali	Also Kalika, literally 'the black one'. Shakti of Shiva in a 'terrify-ing' form; is depicted dancing or in yab-yum with Shiva. Sometimes fused with Durga: Kali-Durga.
Kali Yuga	'Black time'; the last of the four world ages at the end of which Kalki will appear as the last avatar of Vishnu.
Kalki	The tenth avatar of Vishnu who will appear at the end of the present world-age (Kali Yuga) to usher in a new world-age.
Karma	Literally 'action': 1. physical or spiritual action; 2. the consequence of a physical or spiritual action; 3. the sum of all the consequences of individual actions in this or a past

life; 4. chain of cause and effect in the moral world; karma is the driving force behind rebirths.

Krishna	Literally 'dark blue'; the eighth avatar of Vishnu; divine hero in the Bhagavad Gita; popular ishta devata in present-day Hinduism.
Kshatriya	Member of the warrior caste.
Lingam	Also linga: the phallus as a symbol of Shiva.
Mandala	Mystical diagram; aid to meditation.
Mantra	Root syllable to which cosmic powers are attributed (e.g. Om).
Manu	Literally 'human being'; tribal father of humankind, stands between gods and human beings, first legislator, proclaimer of the divine order. Laws of Manu: writings of the Brahmanic period which among other things define the subordinate position of women to men, and also the absolute priority of the Brahman caste.
Matsya	Literally 'fish'; avatar of Vishnu, figure from the Indian flood saga.
Maya	Literally 'deception', 'illusion'; maya coincides with Brahman but belongs to him as heat to fire; maya is also the shakti, the driving force of the Absolute; Brahman and maya combine to form Ishvara, ishta devata, the 'personal god'.

Moksha	Liberation from all worldly ties; karma then has no object and there is no rebirth.
Nandi	Symbolic animal (symbolic mount) of Shiva; representation of a bull, usually of a milky-white colour.
Narayan	Name for Vishnu.
Nataraja	'Lord', 'Prince'; Shiva as 'king of the dancers': as 'Lord of the world stages' he dances the cosmic dance in his five activities of creation, preservation, destruction, embodiment and liberation.
Nirvana	Literally 'extinction'; state of liberation and enlightenment, the taking up of the indivdiual self into Brahman; state of non-duality (also Brahman-nirvana). Nirvana is also a term in Buddhism with insignificant philosophical differences from Hinduism.
Pariah	'Untouchable', regarded as unclean; Pariahs represent the majority of the Indian population; their lot has slowly improved since Mahatma Gandhi (Harijan).
Parvati	Literally 'belonging to the mountain', a shakti of Shiva, mother of Ganesha.
Pashupati	Shiva in his aspect as 'lord of the animals'.
Prakriti	Literally 'nature', 'matter', the primal material of the universe, which is determined by three gunas: tamas, heavy and immov-

able; rajas, activity; sattva, the pure. If the three gunas are unbalanced the manifestation of creation is the result.

Puja

Ritual offering, usually of flowers, fruit and grains of corn; incense sticks are lit or fire is kindled; water is also often offered ritually, mantras and hymns are recited and the sacrificial bell (ghanta) is rung.

Purusha

Literally 'human being', denotes the original, the eternal in human beings, and is sometimes identified with atman.

Rama

The seventh avatar of Vishnu, hero of the Ramayana; Rama and his consort Sita (furrow) are regarded as ideals of husband and wife and are often worshipped.

Ramayana

Life of Rama; Sanskrit epic attributed to the legendary author Valmiki, seven sections with 24,000 double verses.

Ravana

'Demon king' from Sri Lanka, leader of the Rakshasas, the opponents of Rama in the Ramayana. Embodiment of the negative demonic principle, the 'not-divine'; abducts Sita and is defeated by Rama with the help of Hanuman.

Rish

Teacher of humankind, recipient of the revelation of the Vedas, also a general term for 'seer', proclaimer.

Rudra

The 'howling one'; Vedic deity of

	storms and bad weather, the figure of Shiva later emerges from him.
Sadhu	Literally 'having attained the goal'; itinerant and/or begging monk; hermit leading an ascetic life.
Samsara	Literally 'wandering', cycle of birth, life, death and rebirth.
Sannyasin	A man who renounces the world and earthly possessions; his life is uncompromisingly directed towards the attainment of moksha.
Shakti, Shaktism	Literally 'force', power, energy; feminine aspect of the divine essence; 'divine mother', personification of the primal energy, often used synonymously with Tantrism.
Shiva	Deity within the Trimutri; comes from the region of the Himalayas, with Vishnu is one of the most popular ishta devatas in Hinduism. He is also the 'destroyer' and thus maintains the cycles of life.
Shivaites	Also Shaivites. Followers of Shiva, have horizontal stripes on their foreheads. In Shivaism asceticism on the one hand and Tantric elements on the other play a major role.
Sikhara	Temple tower above the garbha griha; symbolizes the world mountain Meru and the axis of the world planes.
Sita	Literally 'furrow'; consort of

	Rama, symbolic figure of female purity.
Soma	Intoxicating juice made from a creeper, drunk by sacrificial priests at certain rituals.
Sudra	Caste of servants and workers.
Swami	Literally 'Master', comparable to the English sir; when put after the name it is an honorific title for 'holy men'.
Tantra	Literally 'web', connection, continuum; a central theme is the divine creative power (shakti) and energy, which is seen in the female principle, the female aspect of God.
Tat tvam asi	'You are that!': the Absolute is the same essence as you. The knowledge of tat tvam asi cannot be attained in an intellectual way as it is spiritual.
Trimurti	'Trinity' of Brahma, Vishnu and Shiva, embodiment of the three gunas.
Trishula	Trident: emblem of Shiva.
Upanishads	Literally opa, 'near to you'; ni, 'down'; and shad, 'sit': sitting at the feet of a guru in order to hear confidential teaching. The Upanishads are the closing part of the Sruti and the basis of the Vedanta, the conclusions drawn from the Vedas. At the centre stand the terms Brahman and atman; but they also communicate apocryphal

	content – in the garb of tales.
Vaishnava	Also Vishnuti: followers of Vishnu or one of his avatars.
Vaishya	Caste of merchants and farmers.
Varna	Literally 'colour', but also 'caste'.
Vedanta	Concluding reflections on the Vedas, a philosophical and religous work.
Vishnu	From the Sanskrit vish, 'effect', one of the three deities of the trimurti; in the course of time fused with Nataraya and Hari. Vishnu is the sustainer of dharma, is incarnate in the form of avatars, when the dharma is in danger of being lost.
Yama	Literally 'self-control'. 1. The first stage in Raja Yoga; 2. the god of death, bears the name 'fulfiller' and 'king of righteousness', is also understood as the judge of the dead.
Yoga	Literally 'yoke' (in the sense of linking up with the deity); different schools of Yoga, in the West usually known only as Hatha Yoga (physical exercises). Further schools of Yoga are: Karma Yoga: unselfish action Bhakti Yoga: devoted love of the deity Raja Yoga: royal yoga Kundalini Yoga: Tantric Yoga Jnana Yoga: the way of abstract knowledge.

Yoga is understood as a way to the knowledge of God.

Yoni   Literally 'shoot', origin, 'source', a symbolic depiction of the female sexual organ in Shaktism, often depicted along with the lingam.

For further reading

P. Bowes, *The Hindu Religious Tradition*, Routledge 1978

Jean-Christophe Demariaux, *How to Understand Hinduism*, SCM Press 1996

R. E. Hume, *The Thirteen Principal Upanishads*, Oxford University Press ²1934

Hemant Kanitkar, *The Hindu Scriptures*, Heinemann 1994

V. P. (Hemant) Kanitkar and W. Owen Cole, *Hinduism*, Teach Yourself Books, Hodder and Stoughton and NTC Publishing Group 1995

David R. Kinsley, *Hinduism*, Prentice Hall 1982

Klaus Klostermaier, *Hindu and Christian in Vrindaban*, SCM Press 1970

John M. Koller, *The Indian Way*, Macmillan 1982

Wendy P. O'Flaherty, *Hindu Myths*, Penguin Books 1965

K. Sivaraman, *Hindu Spirituality I. Vedas Through Vedanta*, SCM Press and Crossroad Publishing Company 1989

R. C. Zaehner, *Hinduism*, Oxford University Press 1966